THE INTERVENTIONIST

Nobody knows more about churches than Lyle Schaller. It is as simple as that. The Interventionist *is fresh, original, and deeply insightful. It is must reading for leaders who want to transform churches.*

Bob Buford, founder and chairman, Leadership Network, and author of Halftime

In his finest effort, Lyle Schaller has combined insights from numerous disciplines with thirty-five years of experience as an interventionist. This book becomes the standard for any church leader considering the role of change agent. From cover to cover the book is a goldmine of wisdom.

William Easum, director of 21st Century Strategies and author of Sacred Cows Make Gourmet Burgers

This book is destined as a must read for every church champion of the future.

David Travis, director of the Church Champion Network

This key by the master of all consultants is must reading for those who would make significant contributions to the churches of tomorrow.

Kent R. Hunter, Creative Consultation Services

If you only buy one book this year . . . then you are the wrong person to be reading Lyle Schaller. With The Interventionist *Lyle has proven one more time that no one else can take such a wealth of information, stories, facts, insights, and questions and craft them into a book that leaves the reader at the end demanding just one more book from the master. This is the book that all of us have begged him to write for years, the book that would give us some clues about his system for diagnosing congregations and you will not be disappointed*

Fred Smith, president Leadership Network

Any book that distills the fruit of Lyle Schaller's thirty-five years of churchmanship and consulting would be impressive, but The Interventionist *is exceptional. Valuable information is linked to practical application, making it easy for parish consultants to bring about logical, positive kingdom-building changes in congregational life.*

Russel Chandler, author, speaker, consultant, interim pastor

Clergy, laity, and consultants will find a goldmine of informational nuggets.

Herb Miller, publisher of Net Results, *in Lubbock, Texas*

THE
INTERVENTIONIST

A CONCEPTUAL FRAMEWORK
and Questions for Parish Consultants, Intentional Interim Ministers, Church Champions, Pastors Considering a New Call, Denominational Executives, the Recently Arrived Pastor, Counselors, and Other Intentional Interventionists in Congregational Life

Lyle E. Schaller

ABINGDON PRESS / Nashville

THE INTERVENTIONIST

This book is printed on recycled, acid-free paper.

Library of Congress Cataloging-in-Publication Data

Schaller, Lyle E.

The interventionist : a conceptual framework and questions for parish consultants, intentional interim ministers, church champions, pastors considering a new call, denominational executives, the recently arrived pastor, counselors, and other intentional interventionists in congregational life / Lyle E. Schaller.

p. cm.

Includes bibliographical references.

ISBN 0-687-05449-4 (pbk.)

1. Church consultation. I. Title.

BV652.35.S33 1997

253—dc20 96-32277

CIP

97 98 99 00 01 02 03 04 05 06—10 9 8 7 6 5 4 3 2 1

MANUFACTURED IN THE UNITED STATES OF AMERICA

To

Charleen

and

Leith

Anderson

Contents

INTRODUCTION

Nine years after I began what turned out to be a long career as a parish consultant, I led my first workshop for people interested in the role of an interventionist. As the years rolled by, and I had the opportunity to work with congregations from sixty different religious traditions, I gradually came to ten major overlapping conclusions about congregational life in North America.

First, the role of a parish pastor is a far more difficult and challenging assignment than it was when I was a pastor in the 1950s.

Second, long-established religious institutions closely resemble other institutions in our culture. One of the common characteristics is a normal, natural, and predictable temptation to try to make tomorrow a carbon copy of yesterday, only better. Another common characteristic is that denial is an attractive alternative to confronting contemporary reality.

Third, the most serious shortage in our society is for skilled transformational leaders who possess the capability to initiate planned change from within an organization. The number one example of that may be the United States Senate. Perhaps the number two example is in institutions of higher education. The United Nations may be the third example. When compared to those three, military organizations possess a much greater openness to innovation and to ideas generated from outside the institution. The demand for effective transformational leaders is increasing at a more rapid pace than the supply—and American Christianity is not an exception to that generalization.

Fourth, in a rapidly changing societal and ecclesiastical context, most religious institutions face a difficult choice. One alternative is to adapt to be able to be sensitive, responsive, and relevant to the personal and spiritual needs of new generations. The second is to be perceived by an increasing proportion of the population as irrelevant. That second choice is compatible with placing tradition high on the list of the driving forces in policy making. The first requires a high level of skill in planned change that is initiated from within that congregation. That resistance to change may be the number one explanation for the fact that the vast majority of congregations founded before 1970 either are on a plateau in size or are shrinking in numbers.

Fifth, for a variety of reasons, societal changes began to surface earlier in Canada than in the United States. Illustrations of that include: (1) opening the gates to large numbers of immigrants from Asia and Central America, (2) national health insurance, (3) the merger of large Protestant denominations, (4) the call for metropolitan government, (5) adoption of the metric system of measurement, (6) crossing a national border for a personal vacation, (7) the erosion of traditional church loyalties among younger generations of Roman Catholics, (8) the effort to preserve rail passenger traffic, (9) regionalism, (10) the demand for official bilingualism, (11) governmental support for Christian day schools, (12) high taxes on motor fuel, (13) foreign ownership of influential components of the media, (14) the flow of private investment across national borders, (15) a remarkable receptivity by long-established Anglo congregations to pastors not born and reared in that country, (16) a broader acceptance of a major role for government (the Canadian constitution affirms the values of "place, order, and good government"), (17) the use of electric "block heaters" in automobiles, (18) a national determination to offset the consequences of increased anonymity by an emphasis on civility and courtesy, (19) the export of electricity across national borders, (20) replacement of the paper dollar with a coin, and (21) perhaps most important of all, an open recognition of the need for religious organizations to earn the loyalty of new generations, rather than to depend on inherited religious allegiances.

One result is that Americans can benefit by going north to examine how the churches can respond to a changing societal context.[1]

Sixth, the differences among congregations are becoming

greater with the passage of time. The safe assumption today is no two are alike. Each congregation has its own unique culture. One reason for that is the decreasing importance of denominational affiliation as a central component of the identity of a congregation. The local community setting has moved ahead of the denominational heritage as a factor in creating that distinctive congregational culture.

Another reason is every year a new record is set in the number of congregations that have been in existence for at least one hundred years.

In 1900 fewer than 4,000, or less than 2 percent, of all religious congregations in the United States could trace their history back for at least a century. At least 80,000 of today's religious congregations in the United States have celebrated their centennial. The passage of time accentuates the distinctive characteristics of a congregation. The longer that congregation has been in existence, the more influential are those local traditions.

One consequence is the need for the interventionist to be exceptionally sensitive to the distinctive culture of that congregation. This often is overlooked by many denominational officials responsible for ministerial placement.

A second consequence is that it no longer is possible to design a program, edit a hymnal, produce a curriculum series, offer a formula for a capital funds campaign, publish an adult Bible study program, train a youth minister, outline the format for a corporate worship service, fashion a church growth strategy, design a staff configuration, or recommend a system of governance that will meet the needs of every congregation. This explains why the interventionist has to customize a strategy for working with each congregation. One size no longer fits everyone! The strategy has to be compatible with the culture.

A third consequence of this trend is that it is becoming increasingly difficult to find a good match between the needs of the congregation seeking a new pastor and the gifts, skills, experience, personality, leadership style, and priorities of the candidate. This trend places a heavier burden on the committee responsible for interviewing candidates. This trend also opens the door for a candidate to accept a greater responsibility for creating a good match. In many situations, the ideal candidate will be a self-identified interventionist.

For the newly arrived pastor, this often means moving beyond the recommended formula of the 1950s of "listening and learning." The new formula for that recently arrived pastor begins with "asking questions, asking questions, listening, asking questions, learning, asking questions, listening, and formulating a tentative agenda."

Seventh, one of the most promising developments of recent decades is the emergence of the trained career intentional interim minister. In many congregations this person comes for six to twenty-four months to (1) serve as the full-time interim pastor, (2) help bring closure to the last pastorate, (3) staff a long-range planning committee, (4) serve as an intentional interventionist, (5) ask questions, (6) take care of the neglected or unfinished business, (7) work with the pulpit nominating or search committee in the quest for a permanent successor, and (8) help prepare the ground for a happy pastorate for that permanent pastor. For many congregations the career intentional interim minister has turned out to be a productive response to the old pattern of a series of three- to five-year pastorates, many of whom were unintentional interim ministers.

Eighth, this erosion of inherited denominational loyalties, and the accompanying decline in the influence of denominational systems, has underscored the importance of that word outside when a congregation seeks an outside third party to intervene. Frequently the desire is for someone outside that particular religious tradition. One example is the increasing number of congregations that seek an intentional interim minister who comes from a different religious tradition. Another is the recent use of Protestant clergy to lead continuing education events for rabbis serving Conservative Jewish congregations.

Ninth, while this statement continues to arouse considerable hostility, one basic societal trend in North America is that institutions, like people, are larger than their counterparts of 1900 or 1945. That generalization applies to grocery stores, elementary schools, medical clinics, stores, commercial aircraft, closets, basketball players, brides, banks, bathrooms, bookstores, universities, hospitals, farms, city halls, law firms, prisons, houses, auto repair centers, highways, parking lots, shoes, airport terminals, motels, the civil service, hardware stores, automobile dealerships, denominational staff—and congregations. The average (mean) size of a congregation today is three times what it was in 1900.

Finally, and this has become the central theme of this book, the most effective way to influence both individual and institutional behavior is to ask questions. The two longest chapters in this book are filled with questions for the interventionist.

The learnings generated by these and related conclusions have led to the writing of five books over twenty-five years on planned change. The first, *The Change Agent* (1972), was directed at the individual who wants to initiate change. The second, *Getting Things Done* (1986), focused on leadership roles and styles. The third, *Create Your Own Future* (1991), was written for members of long-range planning committees. The fourth, *Strategies for Change* (1993), discusses the institutional context for change and offers suggestions on both strategies and tactics. Thanks to God's goodness, a supportive wife, and modern medicine, I have been given the time required to summarize much of what I have experienced and learned as a parish consultant. It took twenty-five years from opening that first file to publication, but here it is! During those twenty-five years, I also had the opportunity to write a couple of other books and edit several by some wise colleagues, but this is the one I have been eagerly waiting to complete. Change is the name of the game, and questions are the heart of that game! That also explains why nine of the twelve chapter titles in this volume end with a question mark and two other chapters are filled with questions.

CHAPTER ONE

Who Are the Interventionists?

After seventeen years the principal of the local high school retires. A new principal comes in and within eighteen months transforms the local culture of that high school.

The family-owned business is sold to a large corporation headquartered in another state. The new owners send a management consultant team in for six weeks to identify the changes that must be made.

Following the eight-year presidency of an aging military hero, John F. Kennedy is elected to serve as president of the United States. He identifies a new set of challenges before the nation.

When Dr. John Harrington retires after thirty years as the senior minister of old First Church downtown, that marks the end of an era. The congregation brings in an intentional interim pastor who is given five assignments, (1) serve as the acting senior minister for two years, (2) complete the process of closure for the era that ended with Dr. Harrington's retirement, (3) serve as the resident planning consultant for that newly created futures committee, (4) decide which paid staff members should be asked to resign or retire and help design a new staff configuration that will be appropriate for that new vision of a new tomorrow articulated by the futures committee, and (5) pave the way for a smooth transition to a permanent new senior minister.

The regional judicatory of this denomination decides that its core purpose is to challenge and resource congregations as they plan for the new day in ministry that includes identifying, reaching, attracting, serving, assimilating, and challenging a new constituency. One of the tools for implementing that core purpose is to provide the services of skilled parish consultants or "Church Champions" to work with the congregations that ask for that resource.

An unusually gifted and experienced minister is asked to become the next pastor of what had been launched in 1952 as a new neighborhood congregation in a newly emerging residential area on the west side of that city. This new mission peaked in size in the late 1970s with an average worship attendance of 183. The next fifteen years brought (1) a succession of three different pastors with three very different approaches to ministry, (2) a gradual decrease in participation, (3) an aging membership as younger generations disappeared but were not replaced, (4) the construction of a badly needed $900,000 meeting room addition in 1982 and (5) the departure of the third of these pastors four months ago.

The number one candidate, a gifted, forty-seven-year-old pastor, was interviewed last night by the call committee. This candidate arrived on the morning of the previous day and spent two days plus the first evening interviewing (1) a half dozen leaders of this congregation in one-hour individual interviews, (2) the pastors of four nearby churches, (3) the city planning director, (4) two different local realtors, (5) a banker, (6) the assistant superintendent of the public school system, (7) the part-time church secretary who had joined the staff in 1973, (8) a dozen leaders from this congregation in an ad hoc two-hour session on the evening of that first day, and (9) the chairperson of the call committee for an hour. (This schedule had been arranged by the call committee at the request of this candidate.)

The meeting last night ran from seven to ten o'clock. The discussion was dominated by the candidate who asked three pointed and penetrating questions for every question raised by a member of the committee. About nine o'clock one of the members of this committee asked, with obviously mixed emotions, "I came here tonight with the impression we were going to interview you and thus far most of the evening has been spent with you interviewing us. I must confess I admire your preparation, but I'm a little concerned about your style. Does this represent your leadership style?"

"This is a matter of substance, not style," replied the candidate. "For the past sixteen years I've served as the pastor of a congregation that has tripled in size and now averages nearly four hundred at worship. Three reasons attracted me to become a candidate to serve as your next pastor. The first is the potential here. I believe the best days in the history of this congregation lie in the twenty-first century. Second, about a year ago I began to feel I was coming to the end of my ministry where I've been serving and I began to look around. Third, my wife's mother lives about ten miles from here, so for family reasons this is an attractive possibility. I asked to come early and to talk with people as part of my effort to discover whether the potential here is as great as I had been told. Now, to get to the point of your question. Yes, I believe I am an initiating leader, so my asking all of these questions is consistent with my leadership style. I did not, however, come here this evening with the expectation that I was applying for a job and would be interviewed by my prospective employer. My goal this evening has been and is to discover what you folks see as the future of this congregation. If your vision matches my gifts and abilities, we need to continue our discussion. If they don't match, we should say our goodbyes and go our separate ways."

Preparation

"I served on two of three of the previous search committees," commented the oldest person in the room. "In both experiences we conducted what in retrospect I would call a beauty contest. What it really boiled down to was that in each case, we picked the candidate with the highest level of competence in interviews. Neither one turned out to be a particularly effective pastor. Both were impressive in the interview process, but what we really needed was someone who could help us redefine our ministry for a new day and also make it happen."

Should the role of the minister who is interested in becoming the pastor of a congregation correspond to the role of a person applying for a job? Or should it parallel the role of the contestant in a beauty contest? Or should it resemble the role of a candidate for an elective public office?

If the candidate feels highly motivated to leave his or her present position and/or is eager to move into that particular pastorate, the answer may be yes to all three of those analogies. In all three the reward system is designed to evoke a positive response from those decision makers or judges.

If, however, the goal is to find the ideal match between the needs of the congregation and the gifts of the minister and/or to further the building of God's kingdom, an appropriate role for the candidate may resemble that of the parish consultant. Both the call committee and the candidate may benefit from this perception of the candidate as an outside third-party interventionist. This role requires the candidate to ask many, many questions. That is an essential component of this process of intervention.

To be more precise, this book is based on six key assumptions.

First, congregations can benefit from the contributions of an outside third-party interventionist.

Second, among those who are called to fill that role are (1) a variety of people on the staff of the regional (or national) judicatories of the various denominations, (2) that rapidly growing number of professional parish consultants, some of whom are full-time staff members of a local pastoral counseling center, (3) candidates to become the next pastor of a particular congregation, (4) the intentional interim pastor who follows the long-tenured pastor and precedes the arrival of the next permanent pastor, (5) the competent minister who spends five to fifty days a year serving as a consultant to other churches while continuing as the pastor or staff member of a congregation, (6) the mentoring team from a teaching church that is helping another congregation prepare for a new era in ministry, and, perhaps most numerous of all, (7) the personally and professionally secure pastor who has concluded, "This congregation is about to complete volume two (or three or four or five) in its history. The time has come to begin to outline the first chapter or two in the next volume of this ministry. How should we go about doing this?" One answer is to invite in a professional parish consultant. Another is to resign and let either the intentional interim minister or the next pastor worry about that. For the creative, future-oriented, competent, and transformational leader, a good answer may be, "I believe I can do it myself."

Third, by definition, the intentional interventionist is willing to accept the responsibility to change the course of history. Instead of reacting to the current set of givens, the interventionist is willing to lead a process of planned change initiated from within an organization.[1] In other words, *interventionist* often is a synonym for change agent.

The emerging role of the interventionist can be illustrated by changes in the practice of law. Once upon a time clients asked their legal counsel whether a proposed course of action was legal. Increasingly law firms now accept the role of interventionist as they seek to help a client find a solution to a problem.[2] The interventionist comes prepared to offer new options that the client had never considered. Frequently these options are presented in the form of alternative scenarios for a new tomorrow with the probable costs and consequences of each scenario spelled out in general terms.

Fourth, the capability to be an effective interventionist is not simply a gift from God. It also includes skills that can be learned.

Fifth, the key assumption in this book is that the number one skill of the effective interventionist combines ten components: (1) the ability to formulate relevant questions, (2) competence in active listening, (3) the ability to articulate follow-up questions, (4) respect for the opinions of others, (5) the ability to offer a realistic and relevant diagnosis, (6) the mind of a good chess player, (7) the competence to suggest alternative courses of action, (8) a skill in challenging people, (9) an eagerness to learn, and (10) a larger conceptual framework for analyzing the data from one particular congregation.

Finally, it is assumed that the capability for reflection also is a crucial quality in the effective interventionist. That often begins with a willingness to examine the baggage that the interventionist brings to each situation.

Chapter Two
What Baggage Do You Carry?

In the early 1980s most physicians, medical clinics, and hospitals received more money if they provided more care for their patients. That was the principle of the fee-for-service system for financing health care. More care produces more income.

In recent years the concept of managed care and capitation payments has reversed that pattern. Under this reward system, less care provides higher net revenues for physicians, clinics, and hospitals. They usually receive a flat per capita payment annually for each patient, so more care means less net income.

Today that is often referred to as a *paradigm shift*.

For approximately one hundred years, from the 1870s into the 1960s, the mainline Protestant denominations in the United States could safely assume that each new generation of adult churchgoers would be theologically more liberal than the previous generation. Frequently the seminary-educated clergy were one generation ahead of the laity in this trend.

Professor Robert Fogel of the University of Chicago has pointed out that a new religious revival began in the 1960s. For the past three or four decades a growing proportion of the new generations of adult churchgoers has been theologically more conservative than earlier generations. Approximately one-third of all American-born residents of the United States identify themselves as religious fundamentalists, but only 21 percent of the adults born after 1960 identify themselves as liberals compared to 32 percent for those born in the 1920–29 decade. The most highly visible evidence of this is the rapidly growing number of theologically conservative or evangelical megachurches largely filled with worshipers born after World War II. Many of these churches either carry no denominational affiliation or are related to an American-born denomination created in the twentieth century. A significant number of these evangelical churches, however, are affiliated with one of the mainline Protestant denominations.

That trend also illustrates the concept of a paradigm shift.

The chief financial officers of today's hospitals must know whether they are operating under the old paradigm of fee-for-service or the new paradigm of capitation payments.

Likewise, the interventionist in congregational life, whether it be a parish consultant or a newly arrived pastor or an intentional interim minister or a denominational staff member will find it helpful to ask three questions. First, is this congregation operating under the old paradigm or the new one? Second, which paradigm do I believe represents contemporary reality? Third, what are the implications when I compare those two answers?

That paragraph illustrates a central theme of this book. More can be learned by asking questions than by giving answers. That paragraph also illustrates two themes of this chapter. First, every interventionist carries intellectual baggage in the form of assumptions, priorities, values, perspectives, and biases. Second, it can be helpful to be more self-conscious of one's own intellectual baggage. This chapter is intended to help you identify some of the baggage you carry.

ARE YOU TRULY OBJECTIVE?

You have been invited to come as an outside third party to serve as a consultant to this congregation. You were told, "We want a completely objective outsider to help us plan for the next five to ten years of our ministry. We believe we can benefit from the perspective and counsel of a disinterested outsider."

What do you say in reply?

The only honest answer you can offer is, "I am an outsider, and I believe I can be of help, but I will not be completely objective. I will bring a value system, an understanding of what I believe God is calling this church to be in today's world, several biases, an understanding of what I believe represents contemporary reality, at least a few earned opinions, and a variety of previous experiences that will color my thinking. Therefore, I cannot promise I will be completely neutral or objective."

This chapter is about the baggage the interventionist carries into a parish consultation.

You have just completed a dinner meeting with the committee that will decide whether or not you should become the next pastor of this seventy-five-year-old congregation. It is now eight-thirty on this Tuesday evening, and you were favorably impressed with what happened during this three-hour meeting. It also is clear that most, if not all, of the members of this committee were favorably impressed with you. Two members of the committee stood out in your eyes as remarkably thoughtful, perceptive, wise, and influential individuals.

As you shake hands prior to your departure, one of these two individuals comes over and whispers, "I live two doors up the street from here. Could you come over to my house for a cup of coffee before you leave?" This appears to be an excellent opportunity to acquire some useful feedback from a wise person, so you accept.

After an hour of informal conversation, this wise member says, "Now that I've shared with you my reflections on our meeting this evening and answered your questions about our situation here, allow me to ask you one question. If you do become our next pastor, and I have a hunch that probably will happen, what baggage will you bring with you? What are the values, the biases, the opinions, the priorities, the perspective on the church and the concerns that you will bring with you?"

Several sections of this chapter are designed to help you analyze the baggage you bring with you to that new chapter in your vocation as a parish pastor or as an interventionist.

What are the most valuable pieces of baggage that you carry with you? From this traveler's perspective that question requires a five-part answer whether the subject is the prospective new pastor, a newly elected bishop, the intentional interim minister, a parish consultant, or a new program staff member in a larger congregation. What are those five pieces of essential baggage?

The first is an unreserved commitment to Jesus Christ as Lord and Savior. Without that you should look into another line of work.

The second is a clearly defined personal belief system. An exception may be the new program staff member who is still in the early stages of defining his or her belief system. For the other three, that personal belief system is the heart of their context for fulfilling their call.

The third is an unreserved conviction that the worshiping community is the number one institutional expression of Christ's church here on this planet. If you hold serious reservations about the viability of congregations in the third millennium, it probably would be prudent to choose another line of work. This does *not* require you to believe that other institutional expressions of the church (denominational systems, homes, colleges, hospitals, seminaries, councils of churches) cannot be legitimate orders of God's creation. All that is stated here is that the worshiping community is number one on your list.

The fourth is a personal conviction that this role is the vocation God has called you to fill. This should not be perceived as a temporary stop on a career path. This role should be perceived as a vocational destination. Once again, serving as a program staff member in a larger congregation may be a legitimate exception to that generalization. Another exception may be the program staff member in a regional judicatory of a denominational system.

The fifth piece of baggage is the central theme of this book and consists of three parts. The first is an insatiable curiosity. The second is an internal drive to ask questions about how it is, and why it's that way. The third is a compulsion to respond to the answer to a question with a new question. The first question is a "how is it" question. The second often will be a "why is it that way" question.

A common example resembles this sequence: (1) What has been the trend in your average worship attendance over the past five years? (2) Why has it been moving in that direction?

(Or why has it remained on a plateau?) (3) What are some of the other factors that you believe have been responsible for that trend? (4) What do you predict the trend will be over the next five years?

THE THREE LEVELS OF DISCUSSION

This introduces a sixth piece of baggage that can be extremely valuable. This one comes in two parts. The first part is to recognize that in many gatherings the conversation often is carried on at three levels. The bottom level consists of facts, impressions, feelings, recollections, hopes, fears, dreams, and predictions. At this level people talk about how it is. "Last year we averaged 143 in attendance at Sunday morning worship." "That was an increase of eleven over the previous year." "I hope it will continue to increase." "I believe we can double that over the next ten years." "I can remember when we called it a good Sunday if we had more than a hundred in church."

At the middle level, the conversation shifts over to perceptions of why it is that way. "The reason our attendance has gone up is we now have a minister who is an excellent preacher." "If we had more off-street parking, we could double in a decade." "The reason our attendance has been dropping is the young families moving into this neighborhood don't seem to be interested in church." This is a more speculative type of conversation than that bottom level.

This is the level at which the interviewer concentrates on the "How come?" questions. Why is it that way? How come attendance plateaued five years ago? How come none of the previous pastors here served more than five years? How come you have few people born after 1960 in leadership positions here? How come nothing has been done to expand your off-street parking? How come your Sunday school attendance has been dropping while your worship attendance has been increasing?

The top level moves to a different theme. Is that good? Is that bad? At this level the comments reflect the values of the speaker. "I wouldn't like to see our church get so big that we didn't know one another." "I believe the ideal size for a church is one that is large enough to attract and keep a full-time resident pastor, but small enough that everyone can feel the pastor is a personal friend." "I think our number one goal should be to make every teenager into a God-fearing Christian who has accepted Jesus as his or her personal Savior." "I believe we should pay off our present mortgage before we even begin to talk about another building program."

Ideally the parish consultant, or the new pastor, or the intentional interim minister will be (1) comfortable with the tendency for conversations to fluctuate among all three of those levels, (2) aware of the level of each answer or comment that is offered, (3) comfortable directing the interview or conversation to the level the questioner wants it to follow, (4) mentally able to sort out these comments and classify them in the appropriate bracket, and (5) comfortable in affirming diversionary comments while keeping the conversation focused on the appropriate level. "That's an interesting and valuable observation, but you've moved our discussion up to that top level of values. Before we pursue that, let's talk some more about how it really is here today or why it is the way it is." In other words the interviewer should persist in keeping the conversation on the appropriate level of discussion. In the early stage of most interviews and meetings, that will be in the bottom level of how it is. Unless there is widespread agreement on the definition of contemporary reality, it will be difficult to reach agreement on a realistic strategy for implementing goals.

It is not uncommon for someone to persist in moving the discussion up to the middle level of "why?" Or to the top level of values. For this outside third party, a useful intervention has been to explain that while growing up on a Wisconsin dairy farm, I observed that cows do not fly. That is a simple bottom level fact. Why don't cows fly? One answer is in the theory of aerodynamics. For most discussions, however, a better answer is, "That's just how it is. Cows don't fly. Let's not waste more time on what we cannot control. Let's come back to the bottom level questions about how it is here today rather than talk about whether it would be good or bad if cows could fly." (Personal observation on values. Since I often fly out of the O'Hare airport, which is just south of a large area of dairy farming, I am glad cows do not fly!)

WHO IS THE INTERVIEWER?

Both the minister who is the candidate to become the next pastor of a particular congregation and the parish consultant usually must make a decision on a common fork-in-the-road question. In this situation, who is the interviewer and who is the interviewee?

A natural, normal, predictable, and defensive response for persons invited to an interview is to grab the role of interviewer.

Your choice is the difference between initiating and reacting. The pastor who is a candidate to fill a vacant pulpit may choose to begin by suggesting, "Before we get to the questions I want to raise with you, let's begin with the questions you want to ask me." This is a courteous initiative. This promises to be a comfortable beginning point for the members of that search committee. This conveys the message the candidate is not a passive personality, but an individual who is both able and willing to direct the discussion. This conveys the impression the candidate is open to questions and is comfortable being interrogated first. This indicates the candidate has come prepared with a set of questions and expects both to be questioned and to ask questions. This also follows the ancient generalization that a good beginning point is to open with the other party's agenda coming first.

In interviews with both individuals and groups in a parish consultation, the outside third party may begin by asking, "Do you understand why I am here and why you are here now? Do you have any questions about what this is all about? Has this been explained adequately?"

After that, the interventionist may next ask, "Is there any subject or issue that you wanted to make sure we talk about? Before we run out of time, I want to be sure we have discussed any agenda you brought with you."

If the interventionist is meeting with a standing committee, it often is useful to begin by asking, "Do any of you have questions about why I'm here or why you are meeting with me?"

"What are the issues and questions you want to be sure we talk about before our time is up?" "Do any of you have an agenda you want to be sure we cover?"

WHO WILL DIRECT THE DISCUSSION?

This introduces a seventh piece of baggage, which is an assumption about human behavior. A safe assumption is that in a group setting anyone who speaks within the first several minutes will be comfortable speaking later, and anyone who does not speak during the first several minutes will be predisposed to continue as a silent and relatively passive listener. The larger the number of people in the room, the more likely that generalization will apply.

One means of countering that normal pattern of human behavior is to encourage everyone to speak at least twice within the first fifteen minutes.

One example of this is when the interventionist meets with a group of adults who joined that congregation within the past six to fifteen months. After raising that introductory question, "Do all of you understand why we're meeting or do you have questions about this?" the outsider could begin with this statement: "The reason I asked for the opportunity to meet with you is that recent new members often share a unique perspective. They do not carry lots of baggage from the past. They bring a picture of what is contemporary reality. They see the present as it really is. Therefore I am eager to hear you describe this congregation to me, but before we get into that, let's go around the circle and I am asking you to respond to three questions. First, tell me your name. Second, how long have you been worshiping here? Third, why did you pick this church? There are lots of churches around here, why did you choose this one?"

This gives everyone an easy and nonthreatening opportunity to speak early in the discussion. The first two questions are objective and easy. A few may find the third somewhat threatening or uncomfortable, especially if they left another nearby congregation where they had become increasingly discontented.

Most, however, find this to be an easy opening set of questions.

The reward for the people in the room is to hear the answers the others give. For some, it is a chance to apply a name to what has become a familiar face. By definition, almost all recent new members who will take the trouble to attend are happy with their decision, so it is an affirming event.

After that first round of questions and responses, the interventionist may ask one of these questions. "From your perspective, what does this congregation do best? Brag to me for a minute or two about what you see as the most significant strengths or assets of this church." Or that second round could be, "Frequently newcomers have questions about why this church does things that way. Do you have any questions about local traditions or customs or schedules or anything else about why it is that way here? Or is there some aspect of congregational life that you would like to see changed?"

After everyone has spoken twice, the participants probably will feel more comfortable talking about more subjective or controversial concerns.

A second example is when the interventionist meets with members of the long-range planning committee or the governing board for the first time. The interventionist wants discussion. If the group numbers a dozen or more, it may be prudent to take the time to ask only one round of questions. "Let's go around the table and please tell me (1) your name, (2) your other major roles or responsibilities in this congregation, such as teacher, choir member, president of an organization, deacon, usher, or treasurer, and (3) the original reason you chose to join this congregation."

If the group is fewer than a dozen, time may permit a second question. "Brag to me about what you believe your pastor does best." Or, "Tell me what your number one wish is for this congregation during the next five years." Or, "If you were limited to one statement, what does this congregation do best?" Or, "What is the number one fork-in-the-road question now facing this congregation?"

WHAT DO YOU BELIEVE?

To help you identify additional baggage that you may carry, it may be useful to reflect on these questions.

1. Do you believe the generational differences among people are worth examining?[1]

2. Do you believe that small churches are primarily miniature versions of large congregations or that there are fundamental differences between small and large churches?[2]

3. Do you believe people choose a church primarily on the basis of physical proximity to their place of residence? Do you believe they should?

4. Do you believe it is easier for a pastor to plant a new mission or to redevelop an aging and numerically shrinking congregation founded before 1950?

5. Which do you believe is the more useful indicator of size, membership or average worship attendance?[3]

6. How important do you believe the teaching ministries are in reaching the generations born after 1955?[4]

7. Do you believe the number of adults joining by letter of transfer is a useful indicator of the attractiveness of a congregation to church shoppers?

8. Do you believe every congregation should seek to represent a cross section of the population residing within a mile or two or three of the meeting place?

9. Do you believe the ideal size of a small group is (a) three to seven persons, (b) eight to fifteen persons, or (c) fifteen to thirty-five persons?[5]

10. Do you believe every congregation can and should experience numerical growth?

11. Do you believe there is a difference between confidentiality and anonymity? Do you believe people will be satisfied if they tell you a secret and you reply, "I cannot keep this to myself, and I cannot forget I know it. This will be a part of the diagnostic process, but I promise you I will not reveal the source of this information"?

12. Do you believe the number one purpose of a first-floor corridor in a church building is (a) to enable people to walk

from point A to point B, (b) to encourage socializing, (c) for internal communication, (d) to provide attractive opportunities for people watching, (e) to separate one activity area from another activity area, (f) for bragging about recent victories in congregational life, (g) for welcoming first-time visitors, or (h) to provide a place to hang cold weather clothing? Your answer will influence how you evaluate the design of a building.

13. Which do you believe is the most effective of these four methods of inviting people to come to church: (a) newspaper advertisements, (b) television, (c) radio, or (d) direct mail?

14. Do you define a "large church" as one averaging (a) over 250 in worship attendance, (b) over 350 in worship attendance, (c) over 500 in worship attendance, (d) over 700 in worship attendance, or (e) over 1,800 in worship attendance?

15. More and more churchgoers are seeking a "full service" congregation that offers a broad range of choices in worship, learning opportunities, the group life, music, and local outreach. How large must a congregation be in today's world to be able to mobilize the resources required for a "full service" ministry?

16. Do you encourage congregations to expand the range of choices offered people, or do you believe that increase in the range of choices often carries an excessive price tag?[6]

17. Which of these do you believe is the most useful *single* indicator in describing a congregation: (a) location of meeting place, (b) date founded, (c) average worship attendance, (d) denominational affiliation, (e) total expenditures, (f) number of members, (g) leadership ability of the pastor, (h) whether it is on a plateau in size or experiencing substantial annual net numerical growth or decline, or (i) age of the volunteer leaders?

18. In evaluating the physical facilities, what is the first room you want to look at: (a) the worship center, (b) the pastor's office, (c) the nursery, (d) the best adult meeting room in the building, (e) the most frequently used women's rest room, (f) the basement, or (g) the parking lot?

19. What do you believe is the ideal tenure for a pastor: (a) three to five years, (b) five to seven years, (c) seven to twelve years, (d) twelve to twenty years, or (e) at least two decades?

20. What is the ideal number of syllables in the name of a

congregation: (a) three or fewer, (b) five or fewer, (c) five to seven, or (d) does not matter?

21. In a congregation averaging 350 or more at worship, what do you believe is the ideal size of the governing board: (a) at least twenty-five members, (b) fifteen to twenty-five members, (c) eight to fifteen members, (d) five to seven members, or (e) one—the senior pastor?

22. Do you believe the term *singles,* when applied to a program category, usually refers to (a) never married adults of all ages, (b) formerly married adults, or (c) both?

23. When a congregation decides to expand the Sunday morning schedule to two worship services, do you believe they should be (a) carbon copies, (b) carbon copies except for special music, or (c) different?

24. When adding program staff, should a congregation usually seek (a) ordained generalists, (b) lay generalists, or (c) specialists?

25. Do you believe there is potentially a strong future for the Sunday school or is it an obsolete remnant from the past?

26. Do you believe congregations should take the initiative in planting new missions or do you believe that should be the responsibility of denominational agencies?

27. What do you believe is the single best way to assess how a congregation nurtures the spiritual journeys of people: (a) to listen carefully to the sermons, (b) to examine the program, (c) to focus on the group life, (d) to listen to what people tell you about their own personal spiritual journey, (e) to ask the pastor, (f) to evaluate the ability of the people to talk about their faith with a stranger, or (g) to attend a regular worship service?

These questions are included here for two reasons. First, to demonstrate that no one is completely objective or neutral. Second, to help you identify some of the baggage you bring when you accept the role as interventionist.

Another approach to this issue of the baggage carried by the interventionist is to reflect on a dozen questions for the parish consultant.

CHAPTER THREE

Twelve Questions for the Interventionist

The outside third party who comes in to serve as the parish consultant to a congregation is faced with several immediate responsibilities. One is to earn and re-earn the trust and confidence of the local leaders. Did they make a wise decision when they invited this outsider in to examine the life and ministry of that congregation? The consultant is engaged in a close, albeit brief, relationship with this congregation. How can that be a fruitful experience?

One way to facilitate that is for the consultant to be perceived as curious rather than as judgmental. A strong case can be made for the argument that the number one characteristic of the effective parish consultant is curiosity. This curiosity usually is expressed by asking questions, but that in itself is not sufficient. The congregational leaders will begin to feel reservations about this whole process unless these questions are clearly both *informed* and *relevant* to this particular congregation.

One way to articulate informed questions is to study the advance preparation that has been completed by the local planning committee well before the arrival of the consultant. This material will include both objective and subjective information. Normally this includes (1) an agenda of the issues to be addressed, (2) statistical data, (3) tabulation of a survey of worship attendance, (4) a brief history of that congregation, and (5) copies of planning committee presentations, vision statements, and reports from previous consultants. (See chapter 11.)

One purpose of this advance preparation is to enable the consultant to suggest a schedule of interviews during the consultation. Another purpose is to enable the consultant to ask for additional advance preparation. A third purpose is to prepare the consultant to ask informed and relevant questions. A fourth purpose is to feed the discovery learning process before the arrival of the consultant.

THE CONCEPTUAL FRAMEWORK

Why would local leaders invite a stranger to come in and intrude on the ongoing life of this congregation? One reason is to benefit from the perspective of an outside third party. Another may be to examine precisely defined issues and questions from within the context of a larger conceptual framework. "We are ready to add a full-time program person to our staff. What should we be seeking?" "If we do, will that require changing the configuration of staff relationships?" "Some of us feel we should remodel this building, while others believe we should relocate. What do you recommend?" "How can we find the volunteers we need to staff our Sunday school?" "In twelve years our worship attendance has dropped by a third. What can we do to reverse that trend?" "We're now an all-Anglo church in a Latino community. What should we do next?" "After thirty-two years here, our pastor is going to retire next year. What should we look for in a successor?" "After ten years, we now average nearly 700 at worship. What changes must we make if we expect to double in size in the next decade?"

These and similar concerns share two common characteristics. First, the local leaders are looking for advice on next steps. Second, that advice should be articulated within the context of a larger conceptual framework. How does one conceptualize that larger picture? My methodology includes asking these twelve questions of myself both before and during that parish consultation. Several of them I also ask of people I identify as informed and reflective individuals.

WHERE AM I?

The most important of these twelve questions can be summarized in three words. "Where am I?" What kind of congregation is this? What are the four or five most distinctive characteristics that will help me identify why this church is different from every other congregation I have ever visited? Is it the size? The place on the growth (or decline) curve? The personality and leadership of the pastor? The level of commitment among the members? The congregational culture? Is this really a European religious subculture trying to reach and serve third- and fourth-generation North Americans or first-generation immigrants of Asian descent? The teaching ministries? The system for transforming believers into disciples? The date when it was founded? The reflections on personal spiritual growth by members? The tenure of the pastor? The commitment level of the volunteer leaders? The system of governance? The approach to the corporate worship of God? The tenure of the lay leaders? The marital status of the members? The real estate? The music? The denominational heritage? The location of the meeting place? Local traditions? The youth ministry? The paid staff? The community context? The location on the theological spectrum? The nationality, language, or racial heritage? The schedule? The level of enthusiasm among the people? The financial base? Internal conflict? The expectations projected of people? The age of the volunteer leaders?

These and a couple of hundred similar questions go through my mind repeatedly as I compare this congregation with other churches I have known. Where does this one fit into that larger comparison base?

WHY AM I HERE?

Whether it be by letter, telephone, or a face-to-face contact, from that initial contact I keep raising my second most important question. Why do you want me to come to your church? What is the agenda you expect me to address? Are the concerns you want me to address within my competence? Why am I here?

The responses to these questions cause me to reject nineteen out of twenty requests. The most common reason for rejecting the invitation is the hope I will come and sprinkle magic dust over a complex problem and cause it to disappear. One common example is the invitation to come and help them do yesterday over again, only better. A second is to come and help put out the fire, but in fact that house burned down four years ago and the fire is now a pile of cold ashes. A third reason to reject invitations is the absence of a clear reason for seeking an interventionist.

These and similar requests are beyond my competence. I simply do not carry that kind of magic dust in my briefcase. I can be most useful if the leaders have clearly and precisely defined their agenda. I want to reserve my time for where I think I can make a positive contribution. That is possible only with a good client.

The second time I ask this question is in examining the advance preparation.

The third time I ask this question repeatedly is after arrival. "Why am I here?" That is a question always running through my mind. In addition to asking myself that question, I always try to ask it of (1) the pastor, (2) if it is a multiple-staff congregation, each program staff member, (3) every volunteer leader who had a voice in issuing the invitation, (4) two or three or four committees, boards, and task forces, (5) the members of the long-range planning committee, if one exists, and (6) each of three or four individuals I identify as wise, reflective, and informed members.

Frequently I express it in these words, "Not everyone shares the same reasons for inviting this outsider to come here. What is your understanding of why I was invited?" After that has been discussed, I ask, "Now, is there anything else you believe I should address while I'm here? Do you have a particular concern that should be on my list?"

WHAT IS MY ROLE?

Overlapping that second question is the one that, if ignored, can produce the most serious misunderstandings. When they asked me to come, what hat did they expect I would be wearing? Occasionally ten different local leaders have ten different expectations of the *primary* role of the interventionist. This can be illustrated by identifying a dozen different roles.

1. The expert in conflict resolution.
2. The church growth expert.
3. The specialist in process.
4. The encourager who finds everyone doing good work, pats them on the back, makes affirming comments, and suggests, "This is something you may want to consider as a way to improve what you are doing."

5. The futurist who will bring descriptions of the effective churches of the twenty-first century.

6. The magician who will sprinkle magic dust around and cause all problems and conflicts to disappear.

7. The diagnostician.

8. The problem solver.

9. The broker in resources who will suggest where they can turn for additional help on specific concerns.

10. The hit man who will cause an unwanted staff member or volunteer leader to disappear.

11. The bearer of relevant experiences who will explain how other congregations have responded creatively and effectively to similar problems.

12. The strategist in planned change who will help them design a ministry plan that will turn today's dreams and wishes into tomorrow's reality.

Which of these roles am I expected to fill? Which of these hats matches my competence, personality, and experiences?

What Can I Affirm?

As I examine the advance preparation, I begin asking the fourth question. What are the strengths, the resources, and the assets of this congregation? What aspects of the life and ministry here can I authentically affirm? What are the strengths that can provide a foundation for building on in planning for tomorrow? I continue to ask myself this question after I arrive. What are the most notable assets here? The pastor? The real estate? Local traditions? Worship? The music? The volunteer leadership? The distinctive local identity? The financial base? The spiritual life of the congregation as a whole? The teaching ministries? The size? The women's organization? The prayer life? The focus on missions? That flood of new members who have joined in recent years? The air of optimism? The large number of leaders born after 1960? The Sunday school? The cell groups? That highly organized and remarkably effective caring ministry? The high school youth? A particular weekday ministry? The clearly defined constituency? Recent victories? One particular staff member? The openness to innovation and change? The quality of the long-range planning committee?

Which are the assets and strengths that can be affirmed without serious reservation?

The responses to these first four questions feed a fifth one that I also ask myself repeatedly.

WHAT DAY IS IT?

This question raises concerns about aging and obsolescence. Every institution is tempted to seek to do yesterday over again.

Back in the post–World War II era, College Hill Church enjoyed the regular participation of nearly two hundred students from a nearby four-year church-related liberal arts college. The college and the church carried the same denominational affiliation. All but one of the college dormitories are less than a half mile from that congregation's meeting place. During the 1970–90 period, the college redefined its role in order to attract new generations of students in what had become a highly competitive market. The denominational identification was downplayed and commuters gradually came to outnumber those living on campus.

As the years rolled by, the membership at College Hill Church gradually grew older and fewer in numbers. In 1987 a fifty-one-year-old pastor arrived to replace the minister who had chosen early retirement at age sixty-three. The average worship attendance during the academic year had dropped from well over 700 in 1962 to under 400. The number of college students in church on the typical Sunday had plummeted from 200 to fewer than a dozen.

This congregation included two dozen leaders who had graduated from that college in the 1946–60 era. One Tuesday evening in 1992, nineteen of them gathered to address this agenda. "What were the reasons we were so attracted to this church back in the 1946–60 era? Perhaps if we can identify what attracted us to this church, we can create a new ministry that will meet the needs of some of today's students." After nearly three hours, this group of adults, most of whom had been born in the 1924–38 era, had prepared a tentative design for a new ministry with undergraduates.

There were three flaws in that design: (1) most of the students living on campus in 1992 were born in the 1969–75 era, not in the 1920s and 1930s, (2) nearly one-half of the 1992 student body were commuters, many of whom were divorced women with part-time jobs and/or with young children at home, and (3) the vast majority of the students either had no active church affiliation or were affiliated with a different religious tradition.

In other words, there was no reason to expect that what had worked with one constituency in 1952 would work with a completely different constituency four decades later.

The parish consultant raises the question, "What day is it here?" Is the ministry plan here designed for 1940? Or 1955? Or 1970? Or 1985? Or for today? Frequently the answer is the ministry plan here appears to be designed on the assumption that next year will be 1959.

The most widespread example of this is the hundred-year-old congregation in rural America that once could depend on farmers as the majority of the membership base. Today the majority of the people living within ten miles of the meeting place are retirees or summer residents or urbanites who want to combine country living with a city paycheck or people employed in recreation and tourism or employees in small factories or in a mail-order business.

A close second in numbers includes the churches that seek to reach the generations born after 1955 with the type of music, the style of preaching, and the worship design that worked so well in the 1950s with adults born before 1930.

A third example is the current youth ministry designed for teenagers born in the pre-1960 era. A fourth is the definition of the constituency as "the people who live within a mile and prefer to walk to church." A fifth is the expectation that self-identified African Americans will come to a European-heritage, Anglo church. A sixth consists of the denominational leaders who oppose Christian day schools because they are all racist academies. A seventh is the building committee that is convinced that people prefer oak pews to theater-type seating or detached chairs while engaged in the corporate worship of God. An eighth includes the advocates of "architectural evangelism" who are convinced if "we build a new building, the people will come." A ninth example consists of those who believe a comprehensive program of adult Bible study can be offered in fifty-minute Sunday school classes. A tenth is the trustee or building committee member who is convinced "a basement offers adequate and low cost space for fellowship and teaching ministries."

These are but a few of the reasons for the consultant to ask, "What day is it here?"

SYMPTOMS OR PROBLEMS?

A teenager goes to the doctor to complain of a pain in the side. After examining the X rays, the physician declares, "The reason for your pain is that you have a broken rib."

The symptom sparks a request for the advice of an outside third party. That produces a diagnosis. Effective treatment can come only after an accurate diagnosis.

The parish consultant receives a thick flow of complaints, wishes, hopes, suggestions, gripes, statistical data, impressions, reflections, and other symptoms. At least a few of these accompany that original invitation. Others surface in the examination of the advance preparation. Most are received during that series of on-site meetings and interviews.

The question that repeatedly flows through the mind of the parish consultant is, "What are symptoms that represent the real issues here, and which ones are really irrelevant static?"

Toward the end of the consultation, I rely on this collection of diagnostic comments to suggest a tentative diagnosis and begin to formulate alternative courses of action and recommendations.

These comments also feed a seventh question I ask both of the people being interviewed and of myself.

HOW COME?

The longer that original list of concerns that the parish consultant was asked to address and/or the larger the proportion of leaders who have been members for more than a dozen years and/or the greater the degree of discontent with the present pastor and/or the lower the ratio of average worship attendance-to-confirmed membership and/or the larger the number of people on the interview schedule and/or the larger the number of pastors who have served this congregation during the past two decades, the greater the probability there will be serious discrepancies among these comments.

These discrepancies evoke the seventh of these twelve questions. This question will be asked in several different ways. When someone offers a descriptive or symptomatic comment that is inconsistent with all other data available at that time, the consultant may inquire, "Tell me more about why you see it that way." The wording will vary with the circumstances, but the point is, how come this statement is inconsistent with all other data I have gathered?

When two basic trends appear to be in opposition, this raises the "how come" question. The church treasurer may be asked, "The average attendance at worship has been declining by about 2 percent annually for several years, but total member contributions have been increasing by an average of 3 percent annually. How come?" When the description of contemporary reality offered by the pastor differs sharply from that articulated by the associate minister or by the four or five most influential volunteer leaders, the consultant asks that "how come" question.

When the reasons for their continued membership here offered by people who joined fifteen or twenty years earlier differ greatly from the reasons offered by recent adult new members, the consultant asks the "how come" question.

When the description of contemporary reality offered by the pastor's spouse differs greatly from that offered by the pastor, that evokes the "how come" question.

When the preliminary diagnosis of the central issues made by the parish consultant differs greatly from the perception of the pastor and/or the most influential volunteer leader, the outsider asks silently, *How come*?

Interviews with the pastor and with many of the mature leaders suggest that one of the leading "bragging points" in this congregation is the exceptionally high quality of ministry with youth. Interviews with a dozen to twenty high school youth surface broad dissatisfaction with the youth program. The parish consultant asks, "How come?"

Perhaps the most frequent reliance on this "how come" question arises when the parish consultant mentally compares this congregation's condition and future with similar churches and concludes, "This one does not fit the pattern. How come?"

WHAT IS CONTEMPORARY REALITY HERE?

If you hope to arrive in Kansas City by six o'clock tonight, your planning for that trip will be influenced by where you are now and the current time. If you are now in Richmond, Virginia, and it is eight o'clock in the morning, you may reach Kansas City with hours to spare. If, however, it is seven o'clock in the evening eastern time and you're still in Richmond, you need to turn to Plan B.

The first seven questions on this list are designed to help the parish consultant accurately describe contemporary reality. That is an essential prelude to evaluating alternative courses of action. You cannot get there from here unless you know where here is.

This eighth question often is the most subjective of any on this list. Everyone knows that beauty often is in the eye of the beholder. Likewise, does this picture of contemporary reality evoke a sense of optimism or a feeling of despair? To a substantial degree, this will be determined by how the parish consultant describes contemporary reality.

First Church reports worship attendance averaged 440 for the past year, down from over 1,200 in 1958 and nearly 700 as recently as 1985. Sunday school attendance has plummeted from an average of over a thousand in 1955 to 300 in 1985 and 185 last year. One-half of last year's total expenditures of $943,000 came from income from the endowment fund. A few months before he died in 1993, a seventy-nine-year-old pillar confided to a friend, "I always hoped my church would outlive me, but I'm afraid it may not outlive me by much."

Is this historic congregation coming to the end of its life cycle?

A second look reveals several recent positive indicators: (1) the average worship attendance hit bottom in 1993 at 317, so last year's average of 440 represents a sharp curve upward, (2) the arrivals of a new senior pastor in early 1994 and a new program director in late 1994 have changed the climate from near despair to something between optimism and euphoria, (3) the fact that the number of small Bible and prayer groups meeting weekly has gone from zero in early 1994 to twenty-four currently is heartening, (4) the average attendance in the adult Sunday school classes dropped from a peak of 485 in 1959 to 58 in 1993, but currently is running close to 90, (5) well over one-half of the adults joining this congregation during the past two years were born after 1960, (6) the combined grades six through twelve youth group averaged 17 in attendance in 1993, but currently the two junior high and the three senior high youth groups report a combined average of 74, and (7) while one-half of last year's total expenditures were financed from income from investments, not a nickel was taken from the principal and the market value of the endowment fund increased by an average of 5 percent annually over the past decade.

Which merits greater importance in describing contemporary reality here at First Church? The long-term trends since those peak years of the 1950s or the developments of the past few years?

More common and less dramatic are those congregations in which the members are aging, but their deep loyalty and commitment to this parish keep the numerical decline to a slow pace. The dollar income keeps rising even as participation drops by one or two percentage points annually. The pastor and many of the long-tenured leaders may insist that "as soon as we can raise the money to pay for a modest remodeling of our building and an expansion of our off-street parking, we will be able to reach dozens of families with young children. The city tells us that during the last three years nearly five hundred new apartments were constructed within two miles of our site. We're convinced that when we have more attractive facilities and more parking, we will be able to reverse this aging pattern."

Is that an accurate description of contemporary reality? Or is that simply predictable denial?

The parish consultant has to decide which data are the most relevant in describing contemporary reality. Frequently one of the most important, and one of the most difficult tasks of the consultant, is to create widespread agreement on one coherent and internally consistent description of contemporary reality. This is important, first as a response to denial and, second, as an essential step in designing a strategy for creating a new future.

WHO DRIVES THE DECISION-MAKING PROCESSES?

While this ninth question overlaps chapter 11 on diagnostic questions, it is one that the parish consultant must ask repeatedly before and during a parish consultation. It first surfaces with the initial contact that leads into the invitation to serve as a consultant. Who issued that invitation? Why did that person issue it? Was the request initiated by a discontented layperson? By the governing board? By the pastor? By a staff member? By a denominational official? By a departing pastor? As part of the call agreement by the new pastor? What does the answer to that question suggest about how decisions are made here?

After arrival, I seek to discover how decisions are made here. Is this a tradition-driven congregation? Does the real estate play an unusually influential role in determining what can and cannot be done? Is the pastor clearly the most influential force in how decisions are made here?

In some traditions the polity is exceptionally influential. For example, the historical context for both Roman Catholicism and The United Methodist Church in the United States is based on the distrust of both the laity and the clergy. Therefore in these two religious traditions, polity is an unusually influential factor in the decision-making processes, especially in defining what cannot be done. By contrast, in most of American Protestantism, the polity is much less of a barrier to change. The big exception to that last generalization is in those traditions where most decisions on such issues as schedules, budgets, the creation of new teaching ministries, and changes in the real estate must be submitted to a congregational vote. This often creates resistance to change and results in watered-down compromises.

Frequently I will ask members I identify as well informed and discerning individuals two questions. The first is designed to surface the names of people who are perceived as initiating leaders, "You wished for a major change here, but you had become convinced it probably could never happen, and so you were on the verge of giving up on this ever happening. One day, however, you discovered that two members here have both come out publicly as strong supporters of this change. When you heard that, you gained fresh hope that this change would happen. If these two members are behind it, that change probably will happen. What are the names of those two members?"

If I have become convinced the pastor is an exceptionally influential leader here, I add a clause to that question excluding the pastor from consideration. "Who, besides your pastor, could . . . ?"

In most congregations one name will be mentioned by seven to ten out of every ten respondents to that question. Two or three other names will be identified by at least one-half of all respondents. When no one name is mentioned by at least one-half of all respondents, this evokes the "how come" question discussed earlier.

The second question is designed to identify leaders who are perceived to have substantial veto power. "Pretend someone here came up with what you were convinced was a totally dumb idea and, to your surprise and dismay, it looked as if it was going to be approved and implemented. One day, however, you learn that a particular individual has come out in complete opposition. You relax because you know if that person is opposed, this new idea will never be implemented. What is the name of that person or persons?"

In reflecting on this pair of questions, it should be noted (1) the power to veto often is easier to acquire and exercise than the power to initiate and implement, (2) long tenure and/or good bloodlines often are more useful in undergirding the power to veto than in reinforcing the power to initiate, (3) usually more leaders are required to initiate than to veto, and (4) these two lists may not have any overlap.

It often is useful to ask the pastor this pair of questions and to see if the names are the same as those given by the most knowledgeable leaders. CAUTION! When these questions are asked of long-tenured ex-leaders, it is not unusual to hear the names of members who once were very influential, but no longer carry much or any influence.

Finally, it is informative to listen, to discover how often "prayer," "the Holy Spirit," and "God's will" are mentioned when leaders are asked about what drives the decision-making processes in this congregation.

This question also is valuable for identifying the answers to the next question.

WHO ARE THE ALLIES?

Why would a congregation invite you to come in to serve as their parish consultant?

The ideal, but rare answer is this, "Everything is going great here! We have no complaints and no problems, and every indicator is positive. We are convinced, however, that the best time to go see the dentist is before you have a toothache. Likewise, we believe the best time to ask an outside third party to come in and help us outline the next chapter or two in our history is when we can plan from strength, not weakness."

At the other end of the spectrum is the congregation in which the parish consultant finally concludes, "It seems to me we have two alternatives here. We can cry over all the opportunities that have passed us by and then pray. Or we can pray and then cry."

Between those two extremes are most requests for outside intervention. The most difficult of this collection display one or more of these seven characteristics.

1. Most of the current volunteer leaders are in a state of denial. The pastor initiated the invitation, but most of the leadership simply "went along with what the pastor wanted." They were not really supportive of inviting an outsider to come in and help. The least attractive of these settings for a parish consultation is made even less attractive when a generous member or a denominational agency offers to pick up the entire financial cost. This reinforces the sense of noninvolvement by the leaders.

2. The congregation has drifted into a state of almost complete passivity. As a last resort the pastor, perhaps with the active support of one or two volunteer leaders, asks, "Please

come in and tell us what to do."

3. After two decades or longer of serving small congregations, this pastor is asked to become the senior minister of a large church. This pastor brings a leadership role and style that fit the small church and imposes them on this large congregation. One result is a gradual erosion in size. Most of the longtime members, however, are delighted with this new senior minister who seeks to become everyone's close personal friend and are comfortable with that gradual numerical decline since one consequence is a reduction in the degree of anonymity and the level of complexity.

4. Opposition to the current pastor is growing. Occasionally the pastor will initiate the request for a consultation hoping this "will prove the pastor is not at fault here." More often several officers and other volunteer leaders initiate the request. After the consultant arrives, the message is sent, "What we really want is not a full-scale parish consultation, all we need is for you to persuade our pastor to resign (or take early retirement)."

5. The pastor may have initiated the proposal to invite in an outside third party and that has received strong support from the governing board. During the advance preparation stage, however, it becomes apparent that the pastor is going to turn over to a planning committee and/or a subordinate staff member complete responsibility for both the advance preparation and the preparation of the interview schedule. After arrival, the consultant discovers that the pastor is committed to a detached or observer role and does not want to participate actively in any meetings with the planning committee and/or the governing board.

6. The parish consultant arrives to discover the congregation is severely polarized with an articulate and determined group consisting of perhaps 10 percent on one side. Opposed to them is another group of equally articulate and determined members. The pastor may be in the middle or the pastor may be on one side of this conflict.

7. The pastor is three or four years from planned retirement. Congregational pressure is mounting for the pastor to resign or to choose early retirement. One way to buy time is to schedule a parish consultation eighteen months in the future. "We can't

do anything until after the consultant has reviewed our situation."

In these and similar settings the parish consultant seeks to identify potential allies who will carry the responsibility for moving from planning and strategy develpment to implementation. Who are the best potential allies here? Ideally the number one ally is the pastor. Ideally the members of the governing board or the lay elders will constitute another group of committed and influential allies. Ideally that alliance also will include (1) the pastor's spouse, (2) several widely respected and influential members who no longer occupy leadership positions, and (3) a dozen or more recent new members who may be part of tomorrow's leadership team here.

Frequently, however, denial and passivity are widespread. Most of the influential volunteer leaders prefer to take a "wait and see" attitude.

One alternative for the consultant is to write this trip off under the admonition, "You can't do a good job for a bum client."

A more constructive response is to seek allies. "It's obvious that some changes must be made here," declares the consultant to a respected and influential leader. "What changes could you support?" This may mean the consultant's final recommendations will be revised from "ideal" to "attainable." Thus the last component of this final question may be, "What compromises are you willing to make in order to enlist the number and quality of allies required to move this visit from an interesting experience to a useful intervention?"

WHAT IS THE CENTRAL ISSUE?

While listed eleventh here, a crucial question is raised from the very beginning of the process to preparing the outline for the final printed report. What is the central issue here?

The most common answer among congregations on a plateau in size or shrinking in numbers is the absence of a clear central focal point for ministry. What is the distinctive quality that distinguishes this congregation from all other religious congregations in this community? What is the unique or distinctive role?

What is the slice of the total population that this congregation is called to serve? A frequent response is, "We seek to be all things to all people." That is a good statement for the worldwide universal church, but that is far beyond the capability of any one congregation.

This absence of clarity on role or lack of focus makes it difficult to order priorities in the allocation of scarce priorities including the pastor's time.

In other situations, that central issue may be real estate or an inadequate financial base or staffing or some other means-to-an-end issue.

Without a clear definition of that central issue, it is difficult to formulate recommended courses of action.

WHAT DO I RECOMMEND?

The purpose of this chapter is to suggest a series of questions that will be running through the consultant's mind before and during that parish consultation. Perhaps the most subjective of these questions concerns the recommendations that will emerge from this process.

A frequent temptation is to overload the congregation with two or three dozen different recommendations. If the goal of the outside interventionist is to make a difference, it may be wiser to keep that list to a couple of major recommendations.

In retrospect, one of my most successful interventions came back in 1982 when I offered two recommendations. First, yes, you must relocate your meeting place. Second, instead of choosing between those two adjacent parcels of land for a relocation site, purchase both of them.

As a general rule, two recommendations are better than four, four are better than eight, and eight is too many. One alternative is to keep the list of recommendations to a small single digit number. This list can be supplemented by a list of suggestions and a list of concerns that merit consideration.

Long ago this interventionist became convinced of the value of offering choices. Thus the central or number one recommendation may be an argument for abandoning the status quo and offering three or four alternative courses of action.

In many institutionally strong congregations, and especially in thousands of small churches, it may be useful to identify five to fifteen potential scenarios for a new tomorrow. One may require modest changes. Several may require substantial changes, and a couple may require radical changes. The question becomes one of degree of change. How much change can this congregation tolerate?

The second half of that approach requires suggestions on formulating the criteria that will enable the leaders to make an informed choice from among the various scenarios for a new tomorrow.

The first recommendation urges the leaders to expand that list of criteria and to rank the criteria in order of importance.

The second recommendation is to expand that list of alternative scenarios, making sure to add the probable consequences of each course of action.

The third and last recommendation is to apply those criteria in choosing from among those scenarios.

In many other congregations the recommendations are ranked. If you feel you can make only one change, your consultant recommends why this be that one change.

In other congregations the recommendations are divided into two groups. The first consists of the one or two or three most urgent concerns. ("Purchase that adjacent property while it is available at a fair price!") The second list includes the recommendations that are important, but may not be urgent.

Throughout the parish consultation the outside third party is reflecting on questions such as these. What is the number one change required here? What format will I use in submitting recommendations? How many can I offer without overloading the system? What compromises will be required to gain the support required for implementation? What do I move down to the category of suggestions and comments? What do I emphasize in the oral report and what do I reserve for mention in the printed report? Which ones do I try out on the pastor before that oral report meeting with the governing board or the planning committee? Which potential recommendations will need widespread support? Which require the support of only a few key people?

This process means that one of the qualities the outsider brings to a parish consultation is an above average degree of patience, but that is only one of many desirable qualities!

CHAPTER FOUR

What Do You Bring?

What are the top two burdens on the visiting preacher who is "filling the pulpit" in the absence of the senior minister in this congregation with four or five hundred people in the pews this Sunday morning?

One burden is to communicate the credibility of the messenger. Does this preacher really believe what is being said? The second is a message that is relevant to the lives and spiritual journeys of the people in that room that day. The pulpit no longer automatically conveys either credibility or relevance.

In an excellent book written for professional consultants, Geoffrey M. Bellman devoted twenty-two pages to the need for consultants to balance their lives and their work. Much later in the book he allocates seventeen pages to what consultants bring to their clients. According to Bellman, the top two of what he calls a consultant's "abilities" are expertise and perspective. The other three are authenticity, friendship, and accomplishment.[1]

For those effective pastors who are now parish consultants, perhaps the number one quality they bring to that relationship is authenticity. "I've been there. I sat in the pastor's chair. I know what it feels like to be a pastor." Congregational leaders in general and parish pastors in particular place a high value on that experience factor.

Until recently most lawyers defined their professional role as offering legal advice to their clients and, when necessary, representing their clients in court. They advised their clients on what was legal and what was not legally permissible, and prepared the legal documents that their clients needed. When the client was an individual or a family, the client often perceived this relationship first in personal terms. Can I trust this lawyer? Do I like this person? Is this someone I can confide in, knowing that what I say will be kept secret? Frequently the client placed friendship and trust ahead of expertise in choosing a lawyer.

The same was and is true of many people as they select a physician or a dentist.

In recent years, the practice of law has changed dramatically. The client of the large law firm often is a corporation, not an individual. Many of these corporate clients hire lawyers to be their negotiating agents and to represent them before a variety of governmental agencies. An increasing number of lawyers now identify their primary role as helping to solve their clients' problems.

Today a growing number of architects specialize in working with religious organizations. They help their clients define their ministry, identify future constituencies, rank their priorities in ministry, examine their financial resources and, individually, design buildings to house the clients' ministries.

What does the interventionist in congregational life bring to that relationship? What does the interventionist do? By definition, like the attorney-at-law and the architect, they are expected to bring professional expertise. Like the architect and the lawyer, the interventionist offers advice.

The details of what the intentional interventionist brings will vary greatly, depending on the role, the qualities of the outsider, and the needs of the client. The intentional interim minister, for example, will bring a different basket of resources from that of the parish consultant who comes for a one- or two- or three-day visit.

THE TOP OF THE LIST

For most interventionists in congregational life, however, six qualities rank at the top of the list of what this third party brings to the process.

After three and a half decades of working with congregations, I am convinced the number one quality is the willingness and the capability to earn the trust of the leaders in that congregation. That requires more than simply a high level of professional competence. Among other factors this requires a skill in active listening, a willingness to listen to a lot of trivia, a considerable degree of patience, a continuing focus on the client's agendas—and in most congregations that means a focus on many clients and several agendas. (See chapter 5.)

The number two quality is credibility—and that rests largely on a combination of trust, experience, competence, Christian commitment, character, and authenticity.

The third crucial quality is a genuine openness to a range of diverse opinions.

The task-oriented leaders who perceive the role of the interventionist as someone who will come in and help them solve their problems usually place professional competence at the top of their list. These leaders often place a premium on credentials and the interventionist's record of achievement in past experiences. My experience, however, suggests that professional competence ranks no higher than fifth on this list of desirable qualities.

The fourth quality in the effective interventionist is the mind of a good chess player. A good chess player always looks at the next move in the light of the opponent's probable subsequent moves. A very good chess player frequently is planning three or four moves beyond the immediate decision. This can be illustrated by three examples.

During the meeting with the long-range planning committee, the interventionist listens as a persuasive personality suggests a radical new idea for ministry. Within a few minutes nearly everyone in the room appears to be completely won over in support of this creative proposal. Early in that discussion, however, the interventionist will ask, "How will this change the priorities in your ministry plan that you adopted two years ago? If you allocate resources for this, will you need to mobilize new resources? Or will you shift resources from some other area of ministry?"

While meeting with the trustees, the interventionist is told, "We need to spend $160,000 over the next four years to replace the roof, install a new heating system, and modernize the rest rooms." The interventionist asks, "Does this mean you are making at least a twenty-year commitment to continue in this building as your meeting place? Or do you expect that you can recover most of these expenditures if you decide to relocate and sell this property? Can you raise an additional $40,000 a year to pay for this or will you have to cut back on program or benevolences? Will the city require you to bring the entire structure up to code in order to secure a building permit for these renovations?"

The interventionist discovers shortly after arrival a local argument about cutting back on summer schedule. A minority want to give the choir two months of vacation in July and August and cut back to only one adult class in the Sunday school for those two months. It appears that the majority prefer a three-month summer cutback beginning a week after the end of the public school term and ending the Sunday after Labor Day.

Instead of focusing on the length of that cutback, the interventionist asks, "What is the impression you want to convey to first-time visitors? A lot of families move during the summer vacation. You have been wishing you could reach more of the newcomers to this community. Will a cutback in the summer schedule help make that happen?"

A highly desirable quality in the effective interventionist is the capability and the willingness to raise questions about the future consequences of proposed actions.

In fifth place is the diagnostic capability of the interventionist. That includes the wisdom required to translate symptoms into problems, the ability to recognize common syndromes of congregational behavior (see chapter 8), a willingness to spend more time listening than talking, a set of criteria or benchmarks for evaluating what is happening here, a big inventory of starter questions (see chapter 11), and the creativity to ask the appropriate follow-up questions.

The competence to suggest the appropriate prescription completes this list of the six top qualities for the effective interventionist and introduces the next question about what the outsider brings to that congregation.

WHAT IS YOUR PERSPECTIVE?

Many of the local leaders in a parish consultation place at the top of the list the value of the outside perspective that the interventionist brings to that relationship. This can be described by a half dozen common statements.

1. "We want someone who can help us look at ourselves in the context of what churches similar to this one are doing when faced with similar concerns."

2. "We have been blessed with the resources to be a leadership parish. What are equally blessed congregations doing to fulfill that leadership role?"

3. "Our pastor is about to retire after thirty-three years. We've been drifting into the future for the past several years. We need an intentional interim minister who can help us bring closure to that chapter and also lead us in outlining the first chapter or two of the next volume in our history. It would not be fair to even begin the process of calling a permanent pastor until we have completed those two assignments."

4. "During the past ten years we've doubled in size and we now average close to 400 at worship. We're looking for a new senior minister who has been the number one associate pastor in a congregation two or three times our current size and who will bring the perspective of a large church to our planning."

5. "We've decided our next pastor should be a woman, so we're looking for a female intentional interim minister who can introduce that perspective into a 123-year-old congregation that always has been served by male ministers."

6. "During the past thirty years the population of this community has quadrupled, but our membership has decreased by 20 percent. So we're looking for a church growth consultant."

Every interventionist brings a distinctive perspective to that relationship. What is the perspective you bring? What is the perspective the client seeks? What is needed?

What Do You Do?

"Why should we spend good money to bring some stranger in here? Why can't we solve our own problems? What would this outsider do?" These are fair questions and they deserve an answer. These are also questions to spark self-examination by the interventionist. "What do I do?"

First of all, the interventionist accepts the role and responsibility of serving as an interventionist. This is relatively easy for the parish consultant. It may be more difficult for the denominational staff member who often is tempted to affirm everything and everyone and depart. It may be far more difficult for the intentional interim minister who may be tempted to accept a combination healer-maintenance role. It may be far, far more difficult for the candidate for a vacant pulpit who wants to leave the present assignment and therefore is tempted to act like a candidate in a beauty contest.

Among the responsibilities of the interventionist are these twelve.

1. Accept the role as an active interventionist who brings an outside perspective.

2. Ask questions and listen.

3. Rephrase questions to focus on causes rather than on symptoms.

4. Help the leaders to prepare a common database that can be used to describe contemporary reality.

5. Encourage people to think and to consider new possibilities.

6. Help the leaders to identify and focus on their central or number one priority. What is the core purpose here? To take care of the current membership? To provide attractive employment opportunities for adults? To seek to re-create and perpetuate yesterday? To reach the unchurched? To encourage children and youth to become good Christians? To maintain this sacred meeting place? To offer people meaningful opportunities to come together for the corporate worship of God? To stand out as a witness for Jesus Christ in the larger community? To maintain a denominational presence in this community? To enable people to blossom? To support denominational goals?

In 1991 AT&T paid $7.48 billion to acquire the NCR Corporation as an entry into the computer business. That acquisition diverted the focus of AT&T. Four years later, that giant corporation decided to spin the computer business off as a separate corporation in order to focus on its core role as a communications business.

Too often a congregation places five or six roles at the top of the list and spreads the resources out to support all of them. More often, no thought is given to this issue. The absence of a central focus in ministry makes it difficult to agree on priorities in the allocation of scarce resources, including the pastor's time and energy.

One of the most valuable contributions the interventionist can make is to help the leaders identify the central focal point or the distinctive role of that congregation. This role usually is a must requirement for the intentional interim minister before that congregation can initiate the process of calling a permanent pastor.

7. Seek and enlist allies as change agents.

8. Unless it is ethically or morally impossible, support the ministry of the current pastor.

9. Identify and lift up trade-offs. Accept the role of a good chess player.

10. Expand the list of possible alternative courses of action.

11. Challenge the leaders to consider and undertake what many had thought to be impossible.

12. When appropriate, force people to choose between Change A and Change B, rather than offer the alternative of endorsing a status quo that no longer is viable.

WHAT ARE YOUR QUALIFICATIONS?

What are the ideal qualifications to be a parish consultant? To be an intentional interim minister? To serve on the staff of a regional judicatory determined to place the resourcing of congregations as the core purpose of its future role?

I offer two responses to an extremely complicated question. The first is autobiographical. What have been my most useful and relevant experiences that have benefited me? In rank order I would lift up these twelve.

1. Experience as a parish pastor.

2. Learning to read, that is, experiencing the joy of reading while in third grade.

3. Nearly seven years of experience in municipal government as a planner, finance officer, and researcher.

4. The good fortune of having been born and reared on a farm.

5. An exceptionally supportive, challenging, and affirming experience in 1960–68 as the first director of the Regional

Church Planning Office serving fourteen denominations in seven counties in northeast Ohio.

6. Military service in World War II.

7. A master's degree in American diplomatic history from the University of Wisconsin.

8. Several years as an active lay volunteer in church before going to seminary.

9. Growing up as the youngest child in my family.

10. A seminary degree and a master's degree in city and regional planning.

11. The challenge of Professor Fred Harvey Harrington and Pastor Albert Buhl to write—which forces one to reflect and to systematize one's perspective.

12. Modern means of travel.

My parents, my friends, our children, and my former parishioners would laugh scornfully at that list, discard it, and replace it with a single item. The wisdom to ask an extraordinary young woman in 1945 to marry me. They are right!

What would I recommend as the top credentials for someone planning to become a parish consultant? For most, I would place these at the top of that list.

1. A supportive spouse.
2. A genuine love and respect for the worshiping community.
3. A happy experience as a parish pastor.
4. Skills in active listening.
5. The capability to ask questions.
6. Diagnostic skills.
7. An understanding of the value of an outside perspective.

A graduate degree from a good research university in an area such as organizational development, social anthropology, planning, political science, or institutional behavior can also be a useful asset.

WHAT IS YOUR METHODOLOGY?

How does the outsider intervene in the ongoing life of a worshiping community? The universal answer is, "Not very effectively unless invited." The second answer is, "It depends." The new pastor has a role unlike the parish consultant. The intentional interim minister combines elements of both of those. The denominational staff person usually brings some kind of denomination-wide perspective. The methodology employed should be compatible with and supportive of the role. It will not be the same for everyone. This can be illustrated by looking briefly at the issue of methodology from five different perspectives.

What Is Your Style?

The first perspective may not deserve the word *methodology.* It may be better to refer to it as *style* or *approach*. This can be illustrated by five examples.

One interventionist does it all by mail. A lengthy questionnaire is prepared and every member (or in very large congregations, every tenth member) is asked to respond to all the questions on that form.[2] The completed forms are mailed back to the interventionist, the results are tabulated and fed into a computer, and the computer prints out an interpretation based on a standard program that compares the profiles of the respondents with what is presumed to be the norm. That interpretation is mailed to the client with a page or two of customized comments and recommendations.

Another interventionist combines a standard printed questionnaire (one may be designed for members and one for staff) with on-site face-to-face interviews, and that becomes the database for specific recommendations.

A third interventionist schedules a succession of two or three or four on-site visits over several months. This has the advantage of giving everyone involved time for second thoughts to be fed into the process.

Another interventionist depends largely on a statistical database covering the past two or three or four decades of this congregation's life plus extensive demographic and economic data about the area in which the church building is located. This is a useful approach for the congregation serving a constituency living within a mile or two or three of the meeting place. It is less useful for the congregation seeking to reach 2 percent of the 50,000 people residing within a ten-mile radius of that meeting place, or the regional church seeking to reach 1 percent of the 300,000 residents within a twenty-mile radius.

A fifth interventionist concentrates largely on the distinctive culture of that particular congregation and the probable implications of that culture.

This book is based on a methodology that includes these ten components: (1) a desire to serve only good clients (the definition of a good client is one who (a) is seeking help and advice, (b) is determined to improve the quality and relevance of that ministry, (c) is open to change, (d) includes both the pastor and several influential volunteer leaders as clients, (e) enjoys the absence of divisive internal conflict, and (f) rejoices in a good match between pastor and parish (this definition does not include churches that want to perpetuate 1955 with minor improvements), (2) considerable advance preparation, (3) on-site visits, (4) the asking of hundreds of questions including (a) questions based on the advance preparation, (b) questions based on observations after arrival, (c) questions based on the response to those initial questions, and (d) questions based on the responses to that first round of starter questions, (5) an attempt to identify and describe the unique culture of that congregation, (6) a heavy emphasis on diagnosis, (7) a willingness to offer both recommendations and suggestions, (8) a neurotic fear of creating a continuing dependency relationship between the congregational leaders and the consultant, (9) a conviction that user fees can encourage responsibility, and (10) a conviction that relationships are now more important than roles.

WHAT IS THE SEQUENCE?

Another perspective for reflecting on methodology or approach utilizes a sequential view of the world. For this parish consultant, that sequence can be described in thirty overlapping steps.

Preparation

1. Respond affirmatively only to invitations that suggest that this will be a good client who is committed to making it a productive intervention.

2. Identify the expectations. If the expectations are beyond the interventionist's competence, politely respond, "No thanks!"

3. Request the appropriate advance preparation by the client. (See chapter 11.)

4. Schedule well in advance that on-site visit.

5. Enjoy the benefits of a good interview schedule.

Style

6. Affirm the need to earn the trust of the people.

7. Begin the process of active listening.

8. Display a willingness to listen carefully and courteously to considerable irrelevant garbage.

9. Practice the conviction that accurate and comprehensive information is the most useful initial response to denial.

10. Seek to identify and affirm competent future-oriented leaders.

11. Begin with the initial assumptions that the current pastor is not the heart of the problem and the current pastor will continue there for many years into the future.

12. Act out the commitment to avoid doing needless harm.

Analysis

13. As soon as possible, begin the diagnostic process.

14. Operate on the assumption that repeating the past probably is not on the list of alternative scenarios for the future. (Eventually today's members will move away, drop out, die, or all three.)

15. Make a continuing effort to distinguish between symptoms (including nostalgia and a powerful attachment to the statuo quo) and the real issues.

16. Define the central or basic issues as precisely as possible and narrow that list of central issues to no more than five if at all possible. Ideally only one major central issue will float to the top of the agenda. At this point begin to focus on prescription, but keep redefining that earlier preliminary diagnosis.

17. Recognize that personality conflicts do exist and cannot be ignored.

18. Identify the unique culture of this congregation that distinguishes it from all other churches.

Process

19. Affirm the fact that resistance to change, especially when change will mean displacement, is a normal, natural, and predictable response to new ideas when first presented and should not be misinterpreted as rejection.

20. Persist in a continuing effort to persuade the leaders that the list of alternative scenarios for the future is longer than they believe it to be.

21. Make a redundant effort to persuade the leaders that the wording of the question often is the key factor in winning support for change. (For example, it is obvious that the time has come to expand the schedule to two worship services on Sunday morning. If the local polity requires a congregational vote, what will be the wording of the question? (a) Do you favor or oppose adding a second worship service to the Sunday morning schedule? or (b) Should the new service be a carbon copy of the other service or a different worship experience to reach a new constituency? or (c) Should the new service be at eight-thirty or nine o'clock?)

22. Insofar as is possible, build on local strengths, resources, and assets.

23. Try out potential courses of action on the reflective and influential leaders as early in this sequence as possible.

24. When appropriate, define and offer attractive alternative courses of action. Challenge the leaders to color outside the lines!

25. Win agreement on the criteria that will be used to rank those attractive scenarios or action plans.

26. Identify and lift up the trade-offs. Define the probable consequences of each course of action. Accept the role as a good chess player.

The Larger Design

27. Design a strategy that will enable that congregation to translate the vision or dreams into a detailed ministry plan.

28. Design a plan for mobilizing local resources.

29. If at all possible, provide all the leaders with an opportunity for reflection and second thoughts.

30. As soon as possible after departure, prepare and submit a written report on reflections, diagnosis, and recommendations. The printed word is more reliable than a collection of individual recollections of oral statements!

WHAT CAN YOU DO?

A different perspective for looking at methodology begins with this question, "What can I do to help this congregation?" The next question is, "How can I do that?"

The intentional interim minister may decide, "My biggest contribution may be in staffing a long-range planning committee." The candidate for a call may decide, "My biggest contribution may come out of asking the right questions of the search committee. To do that means I must arrive a day or two before I meet with that committee."[3] The recently arrived pastor may decide, "I need to focus on that one significant change that (1) is overdue, (2) is attainable, (3) will elevate the level of self-esteem among the members, and (4) most important, will shift the focus here from internal unhappiness over the past to optimism about ministry in the years ahead."

The parish consultant may decide that at a minimum, "I will help them (1) develop an accurate common database defining contemporary reality, (2) translate symptoms into issues, (3) formulate the questions that reflect the real alternatives for the future, (4) build a longer list of scenarios for the future than they would build without any help, (5) identify the trade-offs in the decision-making processes, (6) involve as many people as appropriate in this process, (7) suggest the probable future consequences of each potential scenario, (8) enable them to see how other congregations are responding to similar issues, and (9) push the leaders to move beyond wishes and dreams into preparing a ministry plan."

Another interventionist may decide, "I will focus on the process and facilitate what I believe will be a healthy and productive planning process that will enable them to develop their own locally created and locally owned ministry plan."

The parish consultant with several years of experience adds, "I come prepared to suggest criteria, based largely on the experiences of other congregations of similar size and type, that can be useful in evaluating alternative scenarios for the future."

The specialist in interpersonal relationships may focus on creating a new staff configuration that will enhance internal harmony, build on the individual strengths of the various staff members, and improve the level of quality.

A few interventionists are more daring and declare, "My number one goal is to challenge the people to do what they know they cannot do. My number two goal is to enable them to do what they know they cannot do."

At least a couple will suggest, "All I can do is hold up a mirror so the members can gain a clear image of who they are and what their hopes are for the future."

The appropriate methodology for the interventionist will be consistent with what that interventionist expects to accomplish.

WHAT IS THE SYSTEM OF ACCOUNTABILITY?

The methodology of the interventionist also should be consistent with the expectations on accountability. The newly arrived Baptist pastor who accepts the call as an interventionist clearly will be accountable to that congregation in the months ahead. The United Methodist minister is accountable to the district superintendent and/or bishop when appointment time rolls around every spring. One well-known parish consultant expects the congregation to be accountable to him in implementing his recommendations. Another insists he is accountable to the congregation that invited him, but the leaders are accountable to the congregation, not to him, for implementing the recommendations that came out of that visit. A Presbyterian intentional interim minister declares, "I am accountable to the presbytery for what I do as an interventionist."

The methodology followed by the interventionist should be consistent with expectations on accountability.

A LARGER PERSPECTIVE

Ideally the interventionist will be equipped to bring a larger perspective to the process. The intentional interim minister may do this by serving congregations from three or four or five different religious traditions and of different sizes and types plus reading and participating in conferences. The candidate for that vacant pulpit may be an active participant in a national network of pastors from congregations of that size and type. The denominational staff member may utilize research and reports generated within that denomination plus specialized training experiences. The parish consultant may draw on past experiences with a broad range of congregations of various types and sizes. All can benefit from reading that growing array of research studies, reports of parish consultations, and articles in various journals and periodicals as well as books.[4]

Ideally the interventionist will be prepared to preface several comments with one of these introductory comments. "When compared to similar congregations of approximately the same size . . ." or "Other congregations in similar circumstances have chosen one of these alternatives. . . ." or "The congregations that appear to have been most effective in reaching that particular slice of the population usually display at least three or four of these characteristics. . . ." or "In recent years one of the most effective approaches to that issue has been . . ." or "One of the most attractive new ventures in outreach for congregations of your size and type is . . ." or "Other churches that have implemented what you are contemplating have encountered these three . . ."

This larger perspective can feed the fires of creativity in the congregation that is the current client for the interventionist.

What Are Your Criteria?

How much land should be purchased for a new mission? How much by the congregation contemplating relocation?

In 1952 an answer that was widely perceived to be somewhere between generous and extravagant was three acres. In 1968 a common answer was five to seven acres. In 1985 a frequently used yardstick was seven to twenty acres. By 1995 the best answers ranged between ten and three hundred acres.

What are the assumptions and criteria that the interventionist brings to the planning process? Or to the self-evaluation process? The best answer is that those assumptions and criteria (1) reflect contemporary reality, not the 1930s or 1950s or 1970s, (2) possess a solid pragmatic foundation, (3) are compatible and consistent with the value system of the interventionist, (4) can be adjusted or adapted to a unique local context, (5) carry credibility, and (6) are relevant to the local congregational context.

In many cases one particular criterion may be only the beginning point for asking, "How come?" questions. For example, what is the standard for evaluating the annual financial contributions from members? A useful beginning point is to multiply the average worship attendance times $1,000 (in terms of the buying power of the American dollar in 1995).

The treasurer states: "Last year our average worship attendance was thirty-seven and the combined giving of all our members was $29,800. Do you see that as good or bad?" The interventionist silently thinks, "37 x $1,000 = $37,000, but this is well under that figure. How come?" and asks, "What do you pay for total compensation for your pastor?"

The treasurer answers, "We share a pastor with a nearby larger congregation, and our share of the pastor's total compensation is $11,000 a year."

The interventionist silently calculates, "That is less than 40 percent of total member giving," and comments, "Given your local situation, that is a good level of giving."

The following week that same interventionist is working with a congregation that averages 950 at worship, is in the second year of a capital funds campaign to raise $2 million over three years for a badly needed building program, and places a high priority on both world and local missions. The treasurer reports, "Last year the combined giving of all our people including members, constituents, and visitors, for all purposes, including the building fund, came to $2.1 million."

The interventionist silently divides $2.1 million by 950 and comments, "That comes out to approximately $2,200 times your average worship attendance. That's a little less than we would expect for a congregation like this that is in the middle of a big building fund drive. I would have guessed your total giving would be closer to $2.5 million for last year. What is being shortchanged? My hunch is that since you allocate 25 percent of all receipts, exclusive of the building fund, for benevolences, you may be short on money for program staff. Tell me about your staff."

In another setting someone asks, "How much off-street parking do you believe we need?" One answer is in 1995 one off-street parking space for every three seats in the largest room, but by 2010 that should be a one-to-two ratio. Another response is at least seven vacant spaces five minutes after the beginning of your best attended worship service. A third is more than the standards require if you expect all adults will be in both Sunday school and worship and/or if you are seeking to reach young never-married adults and childless couples. A fourth response to that question could be that the quantity is less important than the convenience and the perception of safety.

Someone else asks, "What proportion of our total receipts should go to compensate the staff?" In small churches this may be 50 to 60 percent. In 1996 a common response was the total compensation for all staff (including housing, et al.) averaged out to approximately eight to twelve dollars for each person at worship on the average weekend.

A better answer begins by looking at the total picture. In larger congregations approximately 40 to 45 percent of all expenditures are allocated for staff compensation, 20 to 30 percent for programs including utilities, 18 to 25 percent for benevolences, and 10 to 20 percent for routine maintenance of the real estate. If more than 20 percent of all receipts are allocated to debt service and/or more than 35 percent for benevolences, that often means underfinancing the future of that congregation.

Another person inquires, "What is the normal ratio between worship attendance and membership? For all churches combined in our denomination, it is only 45 percent. What do you think is desirable or acceptable?"

The best answer is, "That depends." In high commitment churches, that ratio often runs between 200 and 500 percent. In congregations that make it easy to join and difficult to have a name removed from the membership roll, it may be 30 percent.

A better question is based on a survey of worship attendance covering four consecutive average weekends. The first point of analysis is to discover how many members attended at least once in that four-weekend sequence. Next, ask how many of those attenders were present on one or two weekends and how many on three or four. In low commitment congregations those who attended only once or twice usually will outnumber those who attended three or four times. In high commitment churches, those who attended three or four times will outnumber, by at least a two-to-one ratio, those who attended only once or twice. This approach avoids that complicated variable of the definition of a member and makes attenders the base line for analysis.

Or occasionally someone will ask, "How many paid staff persons do we need?" For rapidly growing congregations that are effective in assimilating newcomers, the common pattern is the equivalent of one full-time paid position for each one hundred average worship attendance, but most of these will be part-time staff. For low commitment and numerically shrinking churches, a common pattern is one full-time and one part-time staff position for each one hundred at worship.

In other words, quality, competence, and productivity are more important variables than quantity. Therefore the answer to that question may be, "Focus on performance, not on the number of positions."

Finally, someone may ask, "How many choirs do we need?" A common pattern today is one music group for every forty to fifty people in your average worship attendance. Thus the congregation averaging two hundred in worship may have one adult vocal choir, one handbell choir, two children's choirs, one youth choir, and a band.

Once again, a better answer is, "That depends on who the people are you are seeking to reach." If the answer is adults born after 1955, the answer may be one band, three teams of worship leaders, a brass ensemble, and a high school vocal group.

These examples of assumptions and criteria are offered to make a simple point. One single set of standard criteria will not fit all situations!

TWO CAUTION SIGNS

American civil law requires the board members of a for-profit corporation to act on behalf of the stockholders, not the management or the chief executive. The temptation, however, is for the board members to become a support system for the chief executive. A parallel can be seen in the role of the city council or the board of the local library.

A parallel risk may confront the parish consultant. Who is your number one client? The pastor? The governing board? The long-range planning committee who initiated this invitation? God? The congregation as a whole? The universal church? Opponents of the pastor? The next generation of new members?

If the pastor (or senior minister) displays a reasonable level of competence, it is easy for the consultant to conclude, "My number one assignment is to try to undergird and strengthen this pastor's ministry."

Frequently that is widely assumed to be a given for the denominational staff person filling the role of "church champion" or parish consultant.

This means the interventionist must ask himself or herself that central question. Who is my number one client here? It is easy to pretend objective neutrality but be perceived as an uncritical supporter of the pastor.

The second caution applies only to those who work with congregations from several different religious traditions. One of the points advanced later in chapter 7 is that huge differences can be identified between the religious traditions reflecting a European heritage and those that reflect the American frontier spirit. One of these is trust in the people.

Many of the religious traditions built on a European heritage display a basic institutional distrust of congregational leaders in general and of parish pastors in particular. In the extreme form of this institutional distrust, the polity makes it clear that congregations cannot be trusted to (1) examine and ordain candidates for the professional ministry, (2) select their own next pastor, (3) design their own system of governance, (4) decide how many dollars they want to send to headquarters, (5) identify the missionaries they want to support, (6) exercise unreserved control over their own real estate, (7) plant new missions, (8) decide their own position on such controversial issues as human sexuality, foreign affairs, domestic policy, and priorities in governmental expenditures, (9) choose the music and design the worship experiences to reach new generations of people, (10) select the materials to be used in their teaching ministries, (11) determine the compensation of their pastor, (12) identify the congregations with whom they want to cooperate in local outreach ministries, (13) define the qualifications for program staff members, (14) choose their own name, or (15) decide the appropriate age of retirement for pastors.

By contrast, most of the congregations reflecting an American culture display a far greater institutional trust in the leadership of the laity.[5]

This can create a dilemma for the interventionist who is strongly biased in support of lay initiatives and who is convinced this whole process requires a high level of trust in the local leadership. When working with congregations affiliated with a religious tradition built on institutional distrust of the local leadership, what can the interventionist recommend? Is that interventionist ethically free to recommend specific action plans that can be implemented only on a foundation of trust of local leadership? Or is the interventionist ethically obligated to be consistent with the culture of that particular religious tradition? Or can that ethical dilemma be resolved by simply pointing out, "You must understand that what I am suggesting is not consistent with the institutional culture of your religious tradition!"

These two caution signs also introduce the question of what congregations expect of intentional interventionists.

Chapter Five

What Does the Client Expect?

"No one wants advice—only corroboration."
—John Steinbeck

We have two questions we would like for you to address," explained the most influential volunteer leader in this large and rapidly growing suburban congregation founded in 1940. "First, should we relocate from this site to a larger and more accessible parcel of land? Second, if you conclude that we should relocate, we want you to examine the two parcels of land that we are considering and tell us which one to purchase." The request was for a twenty-four-hour visit to respond to those two questions.

At the end of the first hour, it was obvious that this congregation had two choices, either to plateau in size or relocate. The meeting place occupied four building lots in the middle of a residential block platted back in the 1920s. They had acquired two lots down the street, removed the houses, and paved the land for parking. All four of the adjacent property owners, however, were adamant. They would not sell their homes to this congregation.

The two parcels of land under consideration for relocation were adjacent to each other. The fifteen-acre parcel was more visible. The sixteen-acre parcel had the better access from the freeway. I advised, "Buy both of them and relocate," and went home. Subsequently I discovered that approximately 20 percent of the members opposed relocation, 50 percent were open to that possibility, and 30 percent were somewhere between favorable and absolutely convinced it was necessary. I also learned that the senior minister and a half dozen volunteer leaders favored purchasing both parcels of land while the majority of the leaders were convinced that either one of the two parcels would be somewhere between adequate and extravagant. That consultation occurred in 1982.

By 1987 it was evident that all of us were wrong. The congregation relocated to that thirty-one-acre site, constructed new physical facilities, expanded their ministry, contined to grow, expanded their ministry, continued to grow, and had to purchase adjacent property. They needed sixty acres, not thirty-one acres.

What did this client seek? Several of the leaders simply wanted corroboration. They were convinced that relocation was the only prudent course of action. They sought the affirmation of an impartial and experienced outside third party.

Many of these same leaders also sought advice on which of those two parcels of land would be the better relocation site. The senior minister and a few of the volunteer leaders hoped that this interventionist would support the position that most thought to be extravagant—the purchase of both parcels. They wanted corroboration and support.

That brief on-site visit also revealed that several of the long-tenured members hoped that the consultant would recommend against relocation.

No one sought what might have been the best advice—keep looking until you find an attractive eighty- to one-hundred-acre site at an excellent location. In retrospect, that is what this congregation needed.

This incident illustrates several of the expectations that church members project on the interventionist.

MANY AUDIENCES, MANY EXPECTATIONS

The most obvious point is that the typical parish consultation includes many clients, not simply one. One client may be the pastor, a second may be the long-range planning committee, a third may be the governing board, a fourth may consist of the leaders committed to the need for change. A fifth may be those opposed to change. A sixth may be one or two or three heavily involved, deeply committed, widely respected, and highly influential volunteer leaders who are completely open to new ideas. A seventh may be one or two paid staff members with special agendas. An eighth may be the former pastor who retired recently and continues as an influential resident member.

A ninth may be the denominational staff person who recommended that they seek the counsel of an outside third party. A tenth may include two or three or more members who feel that they have been ignored, but expect that the interventionist will be eager to benefit from their wisdom. An eleventh may be the spouse of the pastor. A twelfth may be that maverick personality who has never been able to enlist local support for what appear to be sound ideas. A thirteenth may be the member who is convinced that the interventionist will represent the authentic voice of God. A fourteenth may be the faction who hopes the consultant will recommend the resignation or early retirement of the pastor. The fifteenth consists of those who expect the interventionist will sprinkle some magic dust around and the results will make everyone happy.

While far from a complete list of all potential clients in a parish consultation, that long paragraph does illustrate a central point. Rarely is there only one client!

WHAT ARE FAIR EXPECTATIONS?

Every client brings his or her expectations to this process. The interventionist cannot fulfill every one of those expectations, for many are mutually incompatible. What are the reasonable expectations these many clients have a right to bring with them?

1. The expectation that each person will be heard and listened to with respect. This is easier to fulfill in one-to-one interviews than in group interviews. The greatest difficulty, however, is to listen intently and respectfully to the individual who comes with either a personal fantasy that bears zero overlap with reality and/or an expectation that the pastor should produce two or three miracles daily.

2. The expectation that what is said in confidence will not be attributed to that person. This raises the distinction between anonymity and confidentiality discussed earlier in question 11 near the end of chapter 2. The interventionist may not be able to keep secret an important piece of information ("Our treasurer is embezzling money"), but does not have to reveal the source of that information.

This also means that permission should be secured in advance before quoting anyone directly by name.

3. On many occasions the most difficult expectation is, "Now, you will tell us the truth, won't you?"

Sometimes the interventionist cannot know the truth. Or the interventionist may mix a note of hope in with the truth. Frequently the truth is not an objective absolute, but rather a reflection of what is in the head of the seeker after the truth. The best the interventionist can promise is, "I will be honest. I will place honesty and candor above tact and politeness when I describe my perception of reality here."

4. Congregational leaders have a right to expect the interventionist will bring a fair level of competence in designing strategies for planned change. The need to change, sometimes a greatly overdue need, is the most common motivation for seeking the help of an interventionist. Therefore the interventionist should be equipped to help design a strategy for planned change initiated from within an organization.

5. The client also should be able to expect that, when this can be done authentically, the interventionist will aggressively seek to identify the strengths, the assets, and the resources that can be part of the foundation for designing a new tomorrow.

6. On the other side of the ledger, the client can expect the interventionist to document all criticisms or signs of weakness or obsolescence.

7. The client should be able to expect that the interventionist will at least begin with the assumption that the system of governance does have at least some merit and the institutional subculture does possess some redeeming characteristics. As was pointed out in the closing paragraphs of the previous chapter, that can create a serious ethical dilemma if the interventionist is strongly biased in support of lay initiative and local control, while the institutional culture of that particular religious tradition is organized around a distrust of local leadership, including the parish pastor.

In some situations the parish consultant may decide it would be wise to point out that potential conflict in values before accepting an invitation to intervene.

8. The client also has a right to expect that the interventionist will bring qualities described in the previous chapter including (a) that larger perspective, (b) criteria for evaluating alternative courses of action, (c) the capability to point out probable trade-offs, (d) criteria and norms for evaluation purposes, (e) at least one or two creative new alternative courses of action, (f) the experiences of similar congregations, and (g) some of the probable consequences of a specific course of action.

9. The client has a right to expect the interventionist will distinguish between the major issues and the minor concerns. One congregation received a lengthy report from a consultant that included nearly one hundred different recommendations. The minor items were mixed in what appeared to be a random order with the major recommendations. That congregation had a right to expect the consultant would isolate the half dozen most important recommendations and discuss them in detail. The other ninety could have been divided into a group of a dozen or two suggestions and seventy-plus comments and observations.

10. Finally, the client has a right to expect a printed report, or at least a detailed memorandum that will summarize the diagnostic comments, lift up the key recommendations, and suggest an action plan for the next steps.

The critical issue, however, is to seek to maximize the clarity of the client's expectations before beginning the process of intervention. This is especially important for the intentional interim minister or the pastor who is in conversation with the pulpit nominating committee.

In the ideal world the client will tell the interventionist, "Your performance greatly exceeded our expectations." That can happen!

CHAPTER SIX

What Are the Lines of Demarcation?

The family practitioner identifies a suspicious-looking spot on the left cheek of this thirty-eight-year-old patient. The spot is about halfway between the patient's nose and left ear. "It may be nothing serious," declares the physician, "but just to be on the safe side, I believe you should make an appointment with Doctor Kearny, the dermatologist, and have him do a biopsy." A week later that same physician makes a similar recommendation to an eighty-three-year-old patient with a similar spot in about the same location.

After the reports on the biopsies come from the laboratory, the dermatologist says to the thirty-eight-year-old patient, "There is about one chance in ten that this is a precancerous growth that could turn into melanoma. That would be very serious. Therefore I recommend you go to a plastic surgeon who will remove this and eliminate that risk."

A week later the dermatologist carefully explains the situation to the eighty-three-year-old patient. "There is about one chance in ten that this precancerous growth could turn into melanoma. You may want to play it safe and have a plastic surgeon remove it. Or you may want us to keep a watch on it and see what happens. What's your preference?"

The dermatologist has drawn a line of demarcation between these two patients based on age, health, and probable life expectancy. In a similar manner anyone working with a variety of congregations will be well advised to look at the lines of demarcation that distinguish one group of congregations from another set. This generalization applies to denominational staff, parish consultants, intentional interim ministers, candidates for a call to fill a pulpit vacancy, and others who work with a variety of churches. The usefulness of this conceptual framework can be illustrated by looking briefly at a dozen different lines of demarcation.

1. SMALL CHURCH OR LARGE CHURCH?

The most common of these lines of demarcation is the one that separates the best of the small congregations from that much smaller number of large and very large churches. The best small churches display four or more of these seven organizing principles, (1) they are organized *primarily* around the second of the two great commandments—to love one's neighbor[1] (the usual expression of this relational principle is a network of one-to-one relationships with a long-tenured, extroverted, personable, gregarious, and loving pastor at the hub of that network), (2) while this means the congregations naturally will tend to be exclusionary, in the best of these congregations at least a few leaders are aware of this predictable institutional tendency and will try to encourage inclusion,[2] (3) the members spontaneously display a continuing and sincere effort to express their love for one another both in words and deeds, (4) they offer Sunday school at the first hour on Sunday morning followed by worship and at least 70 percent of the regular worshipers also are involved in the Sunday school—a proposal several years ago to change to a schedule of worship followed by Sunday school followed by worship was rejected because "that would split us into two congregations," (5) there is a sincere and widespread interest in transmitting the faith to the next generations, (6) at least 70 percent of the confirmed members are present for worship on three or four Sundays in the typical month, and (7) the top three criteria for the evalution of the pastor are skill in interpersonal relationships, character, and Christian commitment.

By contrast, the best of the large congregations (1) are organized *primarily* around identifying and responding in a meaningful way to the religious needs of people including nonmembers, (2) are staffed to substitute for that large network of one-to-one relationships a network of small face-to-face groups and/or a variety of programs designed in response to the religious, personal, and family needs of new generations of people, (3) offer people choices in both worship and learning, (4) place a high priority on local missions and outreach, (5) measure the relevance and quality of the total ministry as the number one criterion in evaluating the performance of the program staff, (6) focus more heavily on unchurched adults than on children of members in their efforts to transmit the faith to others, (7) in the vast majority of large congregations, give a higher priority to music than do most small churches, and (8) offer at least one weekend worship experience that is built around persuasive preaching and is designed for those who are in the early stages of a personal religious pilgrimage.

This line of demarcation is not always reflected by the numbers. A few exceptionally high quality congregations are organized around one-to-one relationships and the second of those two great commandments and average between 125 and 350 at worship but only a very few average more than 500 at worship. A common price tag, however, is that the worship attendance-to-confirmed membership ratio often is below 40 percent.

2. Race, Language, Nationality, or Culture?

The most highly visible of these lines of demarcation reflects racial, language, cultural, or nationality differences.

One example in the early twentieth century was the Swedish Lutheran congregation meeting in a building across the street from the building housing a German Lutheran parish. A recent parallel is the congregation composed of American-born black members meeting in a building down the street from the meeting place of a congregation of Caribbean-born blacks.

A growing number of ideologically driven policy makers are determined that these lines of demarcation can and should be crossed in the ministerial placement process. This strategy calls for American-born Anglo pastors to serve African American churches, for African American pastors to serve Anglo-American congregations, for newly arrived immigrant pastors from the Pacific Rim to serve Anglo parishes and similar cross cultural ministerial placements. Thus far, however, few advocate placing Korean-born pastors in an African American church or a Puerto Rican pastor in a Cuban congregation or an African American female pastor in a Korean American congregation!

While this goal can be defended on the grounds of reducing

cultural barriers, it does place a huge burden on the pastor who must live and serve in a different cultural environment.

It cannot be emphasized too strongly that for millions of adults, these are the decisive lines of demarcation. For many blacks, it is race. For immigrants from the Caribbean, it may be nationality. For immigrants from Asia, it may be language or nationality. For immigrants from Mexico, it may be culture. For gays and lesbians, the number one line of demarcation is sexual orientation.

3. Denominational or Independent?

The Census of Religious Bodies: 1906 conducted by the United States Bureau of the Census reported that 1,079 of the 194,497 Protestant congregations counted did not carry any denominational affiliation. These independents reported a combined total of 75,000 members. Ninety years later the number of Protestant congregations had nearly doubled, but the number of independent churches had grown to an estimated 30,000 with ten to fifteen million constituents.

4. Old or New Music?

From the perspective of many churchgoers born before 1956, the most divisive line of demarcation is music. Does this congregation prefer the music (1) created in the religious revivals of the eighteenth century, (2) created in the religious revivals of the nineteenth century, (3) created in the religious revival of the early twentieth century, or (4) composed during the religious revival of the last quarter of the twentieth century? For instrumental music does this congregation (1) prefer the acoustic sound, (2) prefer the electronic sound, or (3) prohibit instrumental music? What is the date used to define "contemporary Christian music"? Is it 1955? 1967? 1976? 1985? 1990? 1995?

5. Members or Strangers?

One of the subtle, but highly significant lines of demarcation among the Protestant congregations on the North American continent separates those that are primarily focused on care of the current members from those making that a secondary concern. This smaller latter group places at the top of their priorities reaching unchurched people. This is reflected in the values and goals that determine (1) the weekly schedule, (2) the responsibilities of paid staff, (3) the design of ministries with youth, (4) the focus of the preaching, (5) the size of the parking lot, (6) the priorities in allocating financial resources, (7) the design of the teaching ministries, (8) the content of their public relations efforts, (9) the length of the worship experience on Sunday morning, (10) the choice of music, (11) the number and variety of attractive entry points for newcomers, and (12) most important, the operational definition of the primary purpose of a worshiping community.

A much larger number of Protestant congregations give a higher priority to transmitting the faith to children of members than to reaching unchurched adults.

6. High Expectations or Low Commitment?

Perhaps the most significant, but one of the most widely ignored, lines of demarcation separates the 20 percent of congregations projecting high expectations of members from the 40 percent of Protestant congregations in North America that are low commitment fellowships and the 40 percent that project midlevel expectations of members. A crude but convenient indicator is that high expectation churches usually report that their worship attendance exceeds their membership. Low commitment congregations usually report an average worship-to-confirmed membership ratio under 50 percent.

7. Tradition or Market Driven?

Overlapping the last two lines of demarcation is the distinction between those congregations in which the decision-making processes are heavily influenced by local, denominational, and European traditions, and those congregations in which the needs of people not active in the life of any worshiping community are very influential in the decision-making processes.

Leaders in the tradition-driven congregations tend to favor interchurch cooperation in doing ministry. Leaders in the market-driven churches tend to be less interested in interchurch cooperation, except in issue-centered ministries, and more likely to accept the fact that many congregations are in competition with one another, in reaching newcomers to that community and the next generation of churchgoers.

Leaders in the first of these two categories of churches often are highly critical of the approach to ministry by the market-driven congregations. Leaders in the market-driven churches often are remarkably open and often eager to learn from the experiences and wisdom of their competitors.

8. Criteria for Ordination?

In the search for a new pastor or in the effort to fill professional program staff positions, one group of congregations gives considerable weight to paper credentials such as academic degrees, ministerial standing, and membership on denominational or civic committees. A different group of churches ranks character, Christian commitment, a clear call from God, and professional competence at the top of the list of qualities they seek in a new pastor or staff member. These four qualities often are followed by skills in interpersonal relationships, experience, marital status, personal religious pilgrimage, place on the theological spectrum, compatibility with the culture of the congregation, and compensation requirements in the evaluation of candidates with academic credentials ranking tenth or lower.

9. Passive or Eager?

At least a few parish consultants contend that this line of demarcation is the most significant of all. Is this a passive congregation that reacts to what others do? Or is it an active congregation committed to creating a new future for itself?[3]

One of the most challenging assignments for the newly

arrived pastor is to attempt to activate the passive church.[4] One of the most exciting and fulfilling experiences for the interventionist is to be invited in to help an active congregation outline the first couple of chapters in the next volume of its ministry!

10. Growing or Shrinking?

One of the two or three most meaningful lines of demarcation separates the congregations that have been experiencing years of numerical decline from those that have enjoyed several consecutive years of numerical growth.

The former frequently display several of these characteristics: (1) strong pressures to make the care of the real estate the top priority followed by care of the current membership, (2) a gradual increase in the median age of the membership, (3) a widespread desire to re-create 1957 or 1977, (4) a hope that today's children will want to grow up to become carbon copies of members born before 1950, (5) a heavy emphasis on the printed word and on the spoken word in communication, (6) a conviction that black and white are the appropriate colors for a Christian community, (7) a focus on a producer-orientation in planning for ministry, (8) an acceptance of the fact that financial limitations will be the number one variable in setting priorities, (9) a preference for traditional church music, and (10) leaders who are convinced that adherence to a sound organizational structure is the key to effectiveness.

By contrast, the numerically growing organization typically displays several of these characteristics: (1) is remarkably open to new ideas and innovation, (2) provides a large and supportive environment for maverick leaders, (3) assumes that quality and relevance in ministry will produce the funds required to pay the bills, (4) is unusually sensitive to the spiritual needs of people on a self-identified religious pilgrimage, (5) places creativity and commitment ahead of tenure and bloodlines in choosing volunteer policy makers, (6) utilizes visual images in all aspects of congregational life, (7) perceives God's creation to be a world filled with color, (8) assumes that tomorrow will undermine efforts to perpetuate the status quo, (9) enjoys leadership that frequently challenges the people to do what many are convinced is impossible, (10) affirms the value of choices, and (11) is more comfortable with an ad hoc approach to an organizational structure than with a rigid system that "follows the book."

11. COMMITTEES OR TASK FORCES?

One of the more subtle lines of demarcation reflects the organizational structure. The tradition-driven congregation that hopes to make tomorrow a continuation of yesterday often is organized with a governing board and a network of standing committees.

By contrast, the congregation that places a premium on innovation, creativity, and a responsiveness to the changing needs of people is more likely to be organized with (1) a changing collection of single-function task forces, (2) two or three standing committees, and (3) a board that accepts the responsibility for keeping doors open to tomorrow, for long-range planning, for facilitating internal communication, for challenging people to do what they know they cannot do, and for setting the basic direction of the congregation, and places a low priority on telling people what they cannot do.

This second group of congregations places a greater value on outcomes than on the organizational structures or on inputs. Instead of beginning with a focus on boards, committees, functions, and role, this second group of congregations concentrates on prayer, learning, discipling, serving, acts of mercy, spiritual growth, obedience to the Word, God's grace, and relationships. This is an especially significant issue for the intentional interim minister!

12. STAFF LED OR LAY LED?

Smaller congregations usually grant a modest amount of power to the pastor and reserve most of the control for the members. Since many of the members tend to want to perpetuate yesterday and to place care of the members and their children at the top of the priorities on the pastor's time, this naturally helps to minimize the size of the small church. This tendency can be strengthened by a series of short pastorates of three to five years.

In larger congregations, and especially in rapidly growing churches, a conflict may exist between those who want to perpetuate lay control and the natural tendency for the staff to acquire more and more power. Many lay leaders perceive this to be the most important line of demarcation on this whole list.

While it is relatively rare, perhaps the healthiest alternative is for the pastor (and staff) to shift the agenda from the issue of control to (1) trusting the laity to do ministry, (2) challenging the laity to do ministry, (3) trusting the laity to initiate new ministries, (4) challenging the laity to implement those new ministries, (5) trusting the laity, and (6) keeping the focus on ministry, not on control or credit.

This rarely occurs without a long pastorate by an exceptionally secure and creative pastor.

The interventionist uses these and other lines of demarcation to answer that question raised earlier in chapter 3 of "Where am I?"

To fully answer that question, however, requires an examination of what may be the most widely neglected line of demarcation, but that requires a new chapter.

CHAPTER SEVEN

European or American?

What do these religious groups have in common? The Church Of God In Christ, The Church of Jesus Christ of Latter-day Saints, Church of God (Anderson, Indiana), Assemblies of God, The Christian and Missionary Alliance, Seventh-day Adventist Church, Conservative Baptist Association, The Missionary Church, Church of God (Cleveland, Tennessee), Churches of Christ, Universal Fellowship of Metropolitan Community Churches, Reorganized Church of Jesus Christ of Latter Day Saints, The Open Bible Standard Churches, Inc., International Church of the Foursquare Gospel, The American Baptist Association, and that growing number of independent megachurches?

One point of commonality is that all of them are experiencing varying degrees of numerical growth when studied over a period of twenty or more years. A second is that all of them can be described as "made-in-America" religious traditions. While they all display bits and pieces of a European heritage, the reliance on the English language and the printed word being the two most highly visible, all five are largely products of an American culture.[1]

It also is not irrelevant to note that the majority of these congregations are west of the Mississippi River. That part of the North American continent east of the Mississippi River originally was settled largely by immigrants from Europe. That part of the continent west of the Mississippi River originally was settled largely by people born in the East who moved westward.

By contrast, most of the older, predominantly Anglo mainstream Protestant denominations in North America share at least ten of these fifteen characteristics: (1) that denominational tradition originated in western Europe or the British Isles, (2) that religious tradition was brought to the United States by persons born and reared in Europe, (3) the early congregations in that tradition were founded in the eastern third of North America,

(4) the denomination still displays an influential European religious heritage, (5) the national headquarters of the denomination is east of the Mississippi River, (6) the proportion of the North American population affiliated with that denomination today is less than it was as recently as 1960, (7) that denomination is planting fewer than one hundred new congregations annually (during the 1880s the predecessor bodies of several of today's mainline denominations started an average of one hundred to nine hundred new churches year after year after year), (8) fewer than 2 percent of the congregations affiliated with that denomination report average worship attendance of 1,000 or more, (9) despite the baby boom of the 1989–93 era, the number of baptisms per 1,000 confirmed members is down by one-third to one-half from the ratio of the late 1950s, (10) the median age of the membership has been rising faster than the median age of the national population (in the United States the median age of the population in 1992 was 33.4 years, up from 28.0 years in 1970), (11) while 40 percent of the American population live west of the Mississippi River, these denominations report only 18 to 35 percent of their members reside west of that river, (12) the majority of congregations in that denomination are meeting in buildings constructed before 1930—back when people walked to work, walked to the store, and walked to church, (13) their theological seminaries reflect a European academic culture, (14) their seminary professors are more likely to spend a study leave in Europe than in South America or Asia, and (15) most of the denominational officials studied and/or spent most of their time as parish pastors in institutions and congregations east of the Mississippi River.

How many of those points of commonality are displayed by your denominational family?

THE HISTORICAL REFERENCE POINT

In reflecting on their origins, one group of Protestant religious traditions in North America looks back to the Protestant Reformation in Europe and see that as their emancipation from Rome. Among their reference points are the teachings of the

European reformers such as Martin Luther, John Calvin, Thomas Cranmer, William Tyndale, Huldreych Zwingli, George Fox, John Milton, John Wesley, and others. Another group perceives the European Reformation to be a temporary break with Rome that eventually will be repaired. The confessions continue to be a rich part of their heritage and a powerful reference point.

By contrast, the "made-in-America" religious traditions look to the Scripture as their basic reference point. Beyond that they turn to the teachings of their American founders for guidance. While observers, such as this writer, often stretch the definition of "Protestant" to include the "made-in-America" religious traditions, many of them have zero interest in being included under that umbrella. Their basic reference point is not to what happened in Europe a few centuries earlier, but rather to what happened in the Holy Land two thousand years ago. Their second reference point is not to the Protestant Reformation in Europe, but to a more recent reformation in North America.

Why Discuss It?

A growing proportion of the churchgoing population, especially those born after about 1942, has been socialized into a religious and social culture that differs substantially from the European religious culture of many religious bodies. The gap between those two cultures appears to be widening.[2] This is one reason why many of the congregations reflecting the European religious heritage are growing older in the age of the members and fewer in numbers.

Perhaps the most highly visible example of this is the Americanization of many adults reared in the Roman Catholic Church. Literally millions of adults reared in a second- or third- or fourth-generation Catholic home have left that faith because of serious disagreements with the policies, pronouncements, and teachings coming from Europe to North America. Large numbers have remained within the Roman Catholic Church while engaging in practices contrary to the teachings from Rome. Americans love the Pope but ignore the messages from the Vatican.

It also should be noted that the "made-in-America" denominations usually are more effective in reaching American-born blacks than are the European religious traditions.

THE BIG EXCEPTIONS

Like nearly every other generalization, this one has exceptions. The highly visible exceptions are those congregations that carry an affiliation with a denominational family that traces its origins back to Europe, but displays only limited evidence of that European religious culture. It is not uncommon for that denominational identity to be omitted from the public name of that congregation. While the pastor has ministerial standing in that denomination, many of those fellow ministers identify that pastor as a maverick who is not completely loyal to that particular religious heritage, or who was not trained by the appropriate approved seminary. It would be easy to list a thousand congregations that fit the "made-in-America" typology. Most either were founded since 1960 and/or have relocated to a new meeting place since 1960. Two good places to look for these congregations are Orange County, California, and the state of Oregon. Well-known individual examples include Community Church of Joy, Glendale, Arizona; Frazier Memorial United Methodist Church, Montgomery, Alabama; Willow Creek Community Church, South Barrington, Illinois; Mariners Church, Newport Beach, California; Lord of Life Lutheran Church, Ramsey, Minnesota; The Cathedral of Hope, Dallas; Church of the Servant (UMC), Oklahoma City; Christ Community Church, Saint Charles, Illinois; New Hope Community Church, Portland, Oregon; Wooddale Church, Eden Prairie, Minnesota; University Presbyterian Church, Seattle; and Saddleback Church, Lake Forest, California.

From a denominational perspective the most difficult-to-categorize religious tradition is the Southern Baptist Convention. Is this a denomination with a powerful European heritage? Or is it largely a "made-in-America" religious tradition? The best answer may be, "Yes."

It can be argued that the migration of Baptists from the British Isles to New England represents the antecedents of today's Southern Baptist Convention. That claim to a European heritage is reinforced by the contemporary division among some Southern Baptists between an Arminian and Calvinist doctrinal stance, but many more point to the Bible, rather than a doctrine originating with a European white male, as the foundation for their personal belief system.[3]

A more persuasive argument, however, is that the Southern Baptist Convention of today is largely an American creation. The American missionary movement, anti-abolitionism, sectionalism, the American brand of revivalism, the impact of the western frontier on fostering a sense of individualism and local autonomy, the affirmation of an entrepreneurial spirit, the concept of powerful state conventions, the importance of formal education, the nineteenth-century movement for institution building, the powerful endorsement of the total separation of church and state, the pioneering work of the Home Mission Board, the Landmark movement, and the Sunday school are among the American influences that have shaped the Southern Baptist Convention of today. From this outsider's perspective, the Southern Baptist Convention qualifies as a "made-in-America" religious tradition. (It is not irrelevant to note that with the exception of the Christian Church [Disciples of Christ], all the denominations usually lumped together under the umbrella "mainline American Protestant" display a strong European heritage. The Southern Baptist Convention usually is not placed under that umbrella.)

The other big and growing exceptions are those Christian traditions in North America that look to Africa or South America or Korea or some place other than Europe as they trace their history back to earlier generations.

Finally, one more word of caution should be added to this discussion of exceptions. There are a few places on the North American continent where broad, sweeping generalizations about the state of contemporary Christianity are riddled with exceptions. From this observer's perspective, the number one exception clearly is British Columbia. The differences between the general culture of British Columbia and the rest of Canada (or the United States) are so great that the classification process would be facilitated if that province would become a separate and independent nation. That would encourage people to assume, "Those generalizations don't apply to us here."

A second exception is south of the border in the state of Oregon. The religious subculture of Oregon is sufficiently unlike the religious subculture of any other state for it to be exempted from most generalizations. It is worth noting that eight of the most rapidly growing religious traditions in Oregon carry the "made-in-America" label. They are the International Church of the Foursquare Gospel, Church of the Nazarene, Assemblies of God, Conservative Baptist Association, Seventh-day Adventists, Southern Baptist Convention, the Church of Jesus Christ of Latter-day Saints, and the independent churches.

WHAT ARE THE DIFFERENCES?

When the interventionist asks that "Where am I?" question raised earlier in chapter 3, it may be helpful to reflect on this line of demarcation between the European tradition churches and those that carry the "made-in-America" label. In other congregations, the parallel question may be, "Is this an Afrocentric congregation? Or a black church? Or an African American congregation? Or a Negro church? Or is this really a 'made-in-America' religious tradition here?"

It is easy to identify dozens of differences, but it should be noted that not all of them apply to every religious tradition nor to every congregation. In addition, it should be noted that some of these also reflect the aging of that institution. That point is illustrated by the third, sixth, seventh, and sixteenth of the distinctions listed here.

1. The first big difference, of course, is in the corporate worship of God. Congregations reflecting a European heritage are much more likely to exalt the first person of the Holy Trinity in the prayers, in the hymns, in the anthems, in the sermon, and in liturgy. By contrast, congregations reflecting that "made-in-America" heritage are far more likely to exalt the second or third person of the Trinity in the prayers, in the singing, and in the sermon.

Sermons in the American culture congregations are more likely to be longer and directed at skeptics and doubters than in the European heritage churches.

2. A close second is that the focus in the European heritage usually is on worship, orthodoxy, and the sacraments. The American heritage churches tend to place a much higher priority on the transformation of the lives of individuals, that is, on conversion.

As James F. White has pointed out, worship marks the clearest line of demarcation between those congregations that reflect the American frontier tradition and those that draw on the common heritage of pre-Reformation Christianity. This latter group is more likely to follow the liturgical year, to rely on a common lectionary in choosing the Scripture lessons to be read on Sunday, to organize around the Eucharist rather than around the Word, to encourage the wearing of distinctive garb by the clergy, and to encourage an intellectual rather than an experiential approach to the faith.

3. At least a few readers will argue that the number one distinction in the American religious tradition is built on a high level of trust in the laity, while the European religious heritage is organized on the principle that only some of the clergy and few of the laity can be trusted.

4. Congregations reflecting that "made-in-America" religious culture usually project higher expectations of people than do the European heritage churches.

5. Congregations reflecting that "made-in-America" religious culture are more likely to plant new missions or to launch off-campus ministries than are the European heritage churches.

6. Congregations reflecting a strong European heritage often follow a producer orientation in program planning. The highly visible example is the church advertisement on the religion page in the newspaper that includes the name of the congregation, street address, telephone number, weekend schedule, name of the pastor, and perhaps a slogan. Staff titles also reflect this producer orientation. Minister of music or minister of education or senior pastor are examples.

The advertising efforts by the "made-in-America" congregations are more likely to focus on the needs of potential future constituents and begin with a question. "Where will you go to church on Christmas Eve?" and "Need help raising your children?" are two common examples. Staff titles often include a reference to the consumer, not to the producer. Minister of family life and minister of customer relations are two examples.

7. When the discussion shifts to a focus on the future, the leaders in the European religious traditions often begin by affirming traditions, past accomplishments, and the importance of that distinctive religious heritage. The leaders in the "made-in-America" religious traditions are more likely to begin this discussion by identifying opportunities, potentialities, and challenges that lie ahead.

8. In the allocation of scarce resources (money, personnel, time, and energy), the current leaders in the European traditions are more likely to place a high priority on keeping the dying institutions alive and/or retaining institutional ties to semiautonomous agencies, while the leaders in the "made-in-America" traditions are more likely to place a high priority on giving birth to the new in response to meeting new needs of new generations. One evidence of this is that parachurch organizations and pastors of megachurches have replaced denominational agencies as the leaders in building a new generation of religious institutions.

9. The leaders in the European traditions tend to feel the need for strong, well-funded, and stable institutions (such as pension funds, colleges, seminaries, homes) while the leaders in the "made-in-America" institutions tend to be more comfortable with risk, with fragile institutions, and with ad hoc organizations.

10. The concept of the episcopacy, which is a heritage of European feudalism, is far more compatible with the hierarchical approach to governance than to the egalitarianism of frontier democracy.

11. The European heritage religious traditions often identify consumerism as a problem or as a barrier to doing ministry. The leaders in the American religious traditions accept consumerism as a fact of modern life and respond to it as a challenge to be relevant to the religious needs of younger generations.

12. Leaders in the European religious tradition often perceive individualism to be a negative value and affirm loyalty to institutional traditions and support for denominational goals. By contrast, leaders in the American religious tradition are far more likely to (a) affirm individualism, (b) reject the belief that "one size fits all" in favor of customizing resources to a congregation's needs, and (c) approve the ministries of the individualistic and entrepreneurial pastor.

13. The number one criterion for the evaluation of a pastor's performance in the European tradition is peer approval. In the American tradition that criterion has been largely replaced by the response of the parishioners and the unchurched. This second criterion is rejected by those who point out that peer approval is the only sound approach to combating heresy.

14. As they seek to reach the different ethnic populations, the European heritage traditions often require ethnic candidates for the pastoral ministry to attend a denominational seminary that reflects a European culture. The American heritage religious traditions usually give greater weight to (a) recognizing and affirming cultural differences, (b) character, Christian commitment, a clear call to ministry, and gifts while downplaying academic credentials, (c) offering any required academic training in the context of the parish ministry and/or in an academic setting built around that distinctive racial, nationality, or language culture and/or by long-distance learning, and (d) accepting the ministerial credentials of immigrant clergy.

Perhaps the extreme example of this difference is in those European heritage traditions that expect a denominational seminary, with a strong European academic culture to recruit and train American-born blacks, Asians, Latinos, Native Americans, and members of other ethnic groups for parish ministry within that denominational tradition.[4]

15. Clergy from the American religious tradition usually are more comfortable with the concept of the megachurch than are the clergy and denominational leaders affiliated with a European religious heritage.

16. Leaders from the European religious traditions often are more comfortable with an acoustic sound in church music and

hymns written before 1960 while the American tradition usually is equally comfortable with the electronic sound in instrumental music in church and often prefers the post-1960 contemporary Christian music.[5]

In addition to these sixteen widely shared and highly visible differences, two dozen other patterns reflect that line of demarcation between the European religious heritage and the American religious tradition.

17. For whom is Sunday worship designed?

European	**American**
God and adult believers.	Skeptics, doubters, new believers, learners, disciples, and children.

18. What are the widely assumed points of commonality among the parishioners?

European	American
Place of residence and denominational affiliation.	Religious needs and place of one's own personal religious pilgrimage.

19. What is the best environment for educating the next generation of the clergy?

European	American
In seclusion from the laity and in a European heritage academic institution.	With the laity and/or in an academic setting reflecting the heritage of the students.

20. What is the primary source of identity in a parish?

European	American
In the denomination, in real estate, and in traditions.	In the ministries of that congregation and in its constituency.

21. What are the basic building blocks for ecumenism?

European	American
The denominational structure.	Congregations and pastors.

22. Where is the ultimate place of trust?

European	American
In institutions and traditions.	In the people.

European	**American**
23. How long is the constitution or book of church order?	
As long as is necessary in order to cover every possible contingency.	Preferably fewer than 200 words.
24. What is the visual image of "the church"?	
Real estate.	People.
25. How many choices should be offered to people?	
Two. Take it or leave it.	The optimum number plus one.
26. What is the dominant theme in the preaching?	
Law.	Grace.
27. What are the key qualifications for ordination?	
Academic credentials.	Character, Christian commitment, the call, and competence.
28. What is the driving force in servicing congregations?	
One size fits all.	Customize.
29. What is the appropriate garb for the clergy?	
Elaborate.	Plain.
30. What is the definition of membership?	
A destination.	A doorway to learning, discipling, and ministry.
31. Where is the appropriate place for the preacher to stand while delivering the sermon?	
Behind the pulpit.	Moving around to enhance eye contact with as many listeners as possible.

European	**American**
32. How do we reach the unchurched?	
Invite them to come here.	Go to them.
33. What is the preferred organizational structure?	
Hierarchical.	Flat.
34. What are the key factors in designing the staff configuration in large congregations?	
Worship, education, and care of the parishioners.	How do we relate to people?
35. Which is the central component of the identity of our religious tradition?	
Polity.	Belief system.
36. What is the preferred vocabulary to use in transmitting the faith?	
The European vocabulary of the faith.	Vocabulary of contemporary generations of churchgoers.
37. What is the preferred route to ministries with low income people or to financing new ministries?	
Subsidized.	Entrepreneurial and self-support.
38. What drives the decision-making process?	
Tradition and permission-withholding.	Vision, mission, and trust.
39. What are the primary roles and responsibilities of the regional judicatories of the denomination?	
To design and offer programs for congregations and pastors, to seek the support of congregations in accomplishing the denominational goals, to	To strategize with congregational leaders and pastors, to challenge congregations to expand their ministry, and to

European	American
service the institutional needs of congregations, to redistribute income and wealth, and to care for pastors.	resource congregations to enable them to implement their strategy.

40. What are the driving forces in the physical design of places of worship?

Western European architecture.	Function, economy, intimacy, convenience, and openness.

Five Cautions

In reflecting on these forty lines of demarcation, five cautions should be raised. First, this list is not offered as a comprehensive analysis, only to illustrate the variety of the lines of demarcation.

Second, life often is filled with "both-and" rather than "either-or" choices. Many seminaries, for example, are very concerned about the call, character, and competence of the students that they graduate, whereas the American-made congregation may not care if the competent leader comes from within or from the seminary. This list does not include a middle ground, and in thousands of congregations that middle ground overlaps both the American and the European heritages.

Third, while those congregations displaying a "made-in-America" religious culture are more likely to be able to attract Americans born after 1955 than are their European heritage neighbors, that distinction can be overstated. One other factor that should not be overlooked is that most of the European religious heritage congregations were founded before 1930 when that was a more popular approach to the faith.[6] During the 1860–1950 era, first–, second–, and third–generation immigrants from Europe were more comfortable with that European cultural foundation for the Christian faith than are their grandchildren, great-grandchildren, and great-great-grandchildren and new immigrants coming from Mexico, Central and South America, the Caribbean, Africa, or the Pacific Rim. The ships from Europe have been replaced by airplanes coming from other parts of the planet.

Fourth, this discussion should not be misconstrued to suggest that liturgical worship in the European tradition is obsolete. It is not! The proportion of North American churchgoers, however, who prefer that formal liturgical worship service has decreased and the number of those who are satisfied with a second-rate liturgical worship service has decreased dramatically. There are still millions of churchgoers in North America who seek the combination of liturgical worship and excellence in quality and relevance. This distinction has even greater visibility in South America than in North America.

Finally, this is but one of many classification systems that can be used. The wise interventionist will ask, "What are the two or three classification systems that will be most useful in helping me to understand the unique personality of this particular congregation?"

Chapter Eight

Seventeen Syndromes

Frequently my seven-year-old son complains that he is thirsty, that he has to urinate more often than is normal, that he's losing weight, that sometimes he has trouble breathing, and that twice in the past three weeks he has had what appeared to be a light case of the flu and had to vomit, but most days he claims he feels fine," explained the anxious mother to a physician over the telephone.

"Bring him in right away!" urged the doctor.

A few seconds after the doctor looked at the boy, he asked the mother, "Does he have diabetes?" A blood sugar test confirmed the diagnosis. Instead of a normal 80 to 100, the boy's level was over 500.

That physician did not simply ask, "Young man, how do you feel today?" He brought a conceptual framework that provided a basis for reflecting on the symptoms described by the mother and evoked that question upon looking at the gaunt face of this youngster. His question was a preliminary diagnosis.

In a parallel manner the experience base of the interventionist gradually creates a list of common patterns of institutional behavior among churches. These syndromes represent a collection of individual symptoms. When taken together, they suggest a preliminary diagnosis that serves as a beginning point for asking more questions. This point can be illustrated by brief descriptions of seventeen common syndromes.

1. The Ex-Immigrant Parish

During the 1880s a group of Norwegian immigrants came to Minnesota and began to farm. As soon as possible they sent back to the old country for a pastor who came and organized a Lutheran parish. A couple of generations later worship began to be offered in both Norwegian and English. Twenty years later the Norwegian service was reduced to once a month and eventually to once a year. In 1973 the parish called a new pastor—who turned out to be of German ancestry. No one on the call committee had thought to check out that detail.

2. THE EX-FARMING COMMUNITY CONGREGATION

Tens of thousands of Protestant congregations were founded in the nineteenth century to serve a farming, mining, or forestry constituency. The four-mile journey to town required more than an hour each way, so this open country church was founded to serve the farmers (or miners) who lived within a mile or two of that white frame building that was located on a rural road. A few years later the cemetery was opened on the side of the hill just behind the church. In 1940 one such congregation included twenty-six farm families. In 1955 that number had dropped to twenty-four. In 1963 it was down to nine plus fifteen households that included no farmers. Today the congregation averages thirty at worship—one-third live in that village four miles away and drive out to church, one family still farms, and the rest are nearby residents who combine country living with either retirement or a daily commute to a city paycheck thirty to forty miles away.

3. THE EX-NEIGHBORHOOD CHURCH

For the first three and one-half centuries of Christianity on the North American continent, it was widely assumed that people would walk to church. Geography was the key factor, next to kinship ties, race, nationality, language, and denominational identity, in determining where people would go to church. For many families geographical proximity even ranked ahead of denominational ties in choosing a church home. Despite the increased ownership of private automobiles, as recently as 1970 hundreds of new missions were designed to serve the residents of a geographically defined neighborhood. The expectation was that this new congregation would serve "the people living west of Highland Boulevard" or "the people living south of 75th

Street" or "the families moving into those new homes north of Madison Avenue."

Concurrently the number of registered automobiles in the United States increased from 119 per 1,000 residents in 1923 to 560 per 1,000 residents in 1993. The total number of all registered motor vehicles (including vans, pickups, and utility vehicles) in the United States in 1993 was 745 per 1,000 population or 1,105 per 1,000 licensed drivers.

Today friendship circles or social networks are determined primarily by one's vocation, employment, hobby, or membership in a voluntary association rather than by the place of residence. One result is that the neighborhood church no longer finds it easy to attract nearby residents.

4. The Old Downtown Church

As recently as the 1950s old First Church downtown could depend on its reputation, excellence in music, superb preaching, and, sometimes, a large Sunday school to draw the newcomers required to replace the members who died, moved away, or simply dropped out.

The suburbanization of the metropolitan population, the decline in public transportation, and the emergence of exceptionally attractive regional churches with an abundance of off-street parking have undermined the traditional role of the downtown congregation as a "flagship church" that attracted the "movers and shakers" in the local power structure. The chief executives of large companies formerly provided most of the volunteer leadership. Their successors are department heads, educators, and civil servants.

5. The Victims of the Denominational Mergers

The 1930–90 era in American Protestantism was marked by a dozen significant denominational mergers. One product of these mergers was the need to create a distinctive identity for the new denomination or risk watching as the membership gradually grew older and smaller.

A second and parallel consequence was the impact on individual congregations. A common pattern saw Congregation A affiliated with Denomination A meeting in a building on this corner. Next door or across the street was Congregation B, affiliated with Denomination B. To a substantial degree the identity and role of Congregation A were heavily influenced by the history, traditions, and identity of its denomination.

Frequently one-half or more of the adult new members received each year were people transferring their membership from another congregation of that denomination. The same was true of Congregation B.

When those two denominations agreed to unite, that wiped out one slice of the distinctive identity of each congregation. These two neighboring congregations, each representing its own religious tradition, now became competitors for newcomers to the community. Typically one attracted the majority of those newcomers while the other congregation grew older in the age of the members and fewer in numbers.

6. THE TWENTY-YEAR SYNDROME

The new mission is planted and that effort is led by a creative, energetic, personable, hardworking, and productive pastor. This new mission is especially attractive to people who enjoy helping to pioneer the new. One year after the first scheduled public worship service, worship attendance averages 135. A year later it is 170 and planning is under way to construct the first unit of that permanent meeting place. By the end of the fourth year, the new congregation is meeting in its new building and worship attendance averages 260. The next several years are devoted to (1) expanding the ministry, (2) welcoming and assimilating new people, (3) raising money for construction, (4) planning and constructing additional physical facilities, (5) enlarging the paid staff, (6) raising money for the next building program, (7) assimilating new members, (8) bringing a new generation of adults into leadership positions, and (9) paying off the mortgage on that last building program.

Two of the cohesive factors that hold this growing congregation together are the presence and personality of that founding pastor and that collection of specific, attainable, measurable, visible, and unifying goals that are attractive rallying points, serve as satisfying criteria for self-evaluation, and create inviting entry points for newcomers.

Somewhere between year fifteen and year twenty-five, two events change the dynamics of congregational life. First, that personable pastor moves on to a new challenge. Second, the final dollar is paid on the last mortgage on the last construction program.

The natural response is to place the search for a new pastor at the top of the agenda, when that process should rank no higher than third. The first priority should be to respond to the change in the role of this congregation. What once was a new mission organized around five rallying points—(1) the personality and gifts of that attractive mission-developer pastor, (2) the excitement of pioneering the new, (3) building a set of new local traditions, (4) highly visible and rewarding goals, and (5) reaching and assimilating newcomers—is now an old church. What is the new role for what no longer is a new mission? Who will define that new role? What are the desirable qualities in a pastor to match that new role?

A second priority is to seek an experienced intentional interim minister who (1) can help bring closure to that first pastorate, (2) understands the nature of the twenty-year syndrome, (3) brings the skills of an effective interventionist, (4) can help the leaders of that congregation define a new role for itself in this post-building stage of its history, and (5) can prepare the way for a happy and effective pastorate by the minister who will be the next permanent pastor here.

Too often, however, that search for a permanent pastor becomes the number one priority. A new "permanent" pastor arrives and quickly discovers that two of the keys to success here are to have seniority on every member and to carry first-hand memories of the past.

A couple of years after arrival, that second pastor departs—happy to be able to depart for greener pastures and leaving behind many people who would have been happier if the termination had come earlier.

Many years later that second pastor realizes, "I came with two handicaps. I came to fill a vacancy that really did not exist. The need was for an intentional interim pastor and I was the unintentional interim minister. Second, I was a victim of the twenty-year syndrome."

WHAT ARE THE POINTS OF COMMONALITY?

Together these six examples of common patterns of institutional behavior illustrate a half dozen syndromes. Each one provides a distinctive context for the diagnostic skills of the interventionist. Each one also illustrates several common issues in designing a new tomorrow.

The most obvious point of commonality is that in all six examples the congregation's past is behind it—and is not a blueprint for tomorrow. The boats are no longer coming over from Scandinavia. The road that led to today will not take that congregation into a new tomorrow. A new road map is needed.

Second, each type of congregation is faced with the difficult choice of change or shrink. Change means redefining the congregation's identity, designing a new role, and identifying a new constituency.

Third, in all six, the power of the past, the appeal of the status quo, and the absence of a widely perceived crisis mean planned change does not automatically enjoy a large and influential constituency.

Fourth, and perhaps most significant, all six examples illustrate the need for a skilled interventionist. Without the impetus provided by a widely perceived crisis, all six syndromes described here usually lead to continued institutional decline. All six illustrate the need for planned change initiated from within an organization. Who will serve as the interventionist to break that cycle? One possibililty is the newly arrived pastor who also is a self-identified interventionist and brings the skills of a transformational leader. A second possibility is the intentional interim pastor who keeps feeding the local discontent with the status quo by asking pointed questions. A third is the outside third-party parish consultant who is both a diagnostician and an agent of planned change. A fourth possibility may be a "church champion" on the staff of a regional or national denominational judicatory. A fifth may be a third-generation member who accepts the role of self-identified interventionist.

Fifth, in at least four or five of these six examples, care of today's members and the perpetuation of local traditions will make it difficult to reach newcomers to that community.

Finally, the future of all six probably will depend on their ability to carve out a distinctive identity and a new role that does not reflect the place of residence of the future constituents.

7. The Price Tags on Rapid Growth

Another common syndrome can be seen in the congregation that has experienced very rapid numerical growth in recent years. One rural congregation celebrated 150 years of existence in 1980. The average worship attendance was thirty-seven for that anniversary year. At its peak in size in the 1920s, worship attendance averaged fifty-three. The first full-time resident pastor arrived in 1982. As the cornfields were replaced with residential subdivisions and retail facilities, that congregation relocated to a larger and more accessible site one mile east and continued to grow. In 1995, it was averaging 470 at worship.

Five hundred miles away, a congregation founded in 1980 with thirty-two charter members was averaging 600 at worship in 1995.

Fifteen hundred miles away a congregation founded in 1955 peaked in size with 300 at worship in 1969. During the next dozen years it was served by a succession of six "permanent" pastors and the average worship attendance gradually dropped to ninety-five. In 1981 the present pastor arrived, and in 1995 the average worship attendance had climbed to 2,350.

All three of these congregations in 1995 were burdened with the same set of price tags on rapid growth.

1. Anonymity had replaced intimacy.

2. Complexity had replaced simplicity.

3. The capability to attract new people exceeded the capacity to assimilate them.

4. The rate of increase in attendance exceeded the rate of increase in contributions of money.

5. The faster the rate of new people coming in, the higher the annual turnover rate as other people left.

6. The need for more physical space exceeded the available financial resources to provide more space.

7. In order to respond to more people with limited space, the weekend schedule was expanded and that increased the level of anonymity and complexity.

8. The role of the pastor changed from "doing it" to "making sure it gets done."

9. The expansion of paid staff required designing a new configuration for staff relationships.

10. The need to expand the group life exceeded the capability of the staff to create new groups that rapidly.

11. The original focus in governance was on representation, but that needed to be replaced by a new emphasis on competence, quality, relevance, and performance.

12. The self-image had to be transformed from a congregation of groups, classes, choirs, individuals, officers, cells, organizations, and fellowships into a congregation of congregations of groups, classes, et al.

13. The senior pastor had to adjust from "knowing all the answers to all the questions" to "knowing who has the answer to that question."

14. The adult Sunday school had to be replaced by a seven-day-a-week assortment of learning opportunities for adults.

15. The arrival of the second preacher, who now preaches at one service on at least forty-plus weekends a year, required a redefinition of the identity and role of the senior minister.

16. The scale of the entire operation has expanded greatly. Formerly the volunteer leader could "keep track of everything in my head. Now I need to bring my notebook or file to every meeting."

17. The system for identifying, enlisting, training, and supporting volunteers has not expanded as rapidly as the need for more volunteers. One result is that the "worker bees" are overloaded while other potential volunteers disappear when they conclude they are not needed.

While not offered as an exhaustive list, those are among the common price tags on rapid growth.

What Year Is It?

Back in the 1950s it was widely assumed that a pastor with a reasonable level of competence could serve effectively in at least nine out of ten churches in that denominational family. That may have been a slightly extravagant hope, but it was not far removed from reality.

One of the big changes of the last half century is the obsolescence of that assumption. Today it is far more difficult to produce a good match between the needs of a congregation and the gifts and skills of a pastor. One result is the emergence of four common syndromes.

8. We Outgrew Our Pastor

The obvious example is the small-to-middle-sized congregation that enjoys a good match between the pastor and the people and is successful in attracting large numbers of new members. By working harder and longer hours, the pastor is able to "keep up" with that influx of newcomers. Eventually, however, the growth requires a change in that pastor's approach to ministry. When the pastor is unable to make those changes, the growth curve flattens out into a plateau. One alternative is to accept that plateauing as normal and continue with that overburdened pastor. A second is to change pastors. A third, and by far the most difficult, is for that pastor to learn how to practice a new role in a new approach to ministry in a larger and more complex setting.

A parallel syndrome often can be seen in the approach to ministry of the pastor who spends two or three decades serving congregations averaging fewer than 200 at worship and then moves on to become the senior pastor of a congregation averaging 350 to 500 at worship. The temptation is to reduce the size to fit the ministry style of that new pastor.

9. The Departure of the Superstar

While less common today than it was in the 1945–90 era, occasionally a congregation experiences rapid numerical growth following the arrival of that creative, ambitious, visionary, and charming pastor who also is a superstar preacher.

Eventually, the superstar leaves and that is followed by a 30 to 70 percent decline in worship attendance.

Why? Most of those worshipers had identified with the superstar preacher. When that magnetic personality disappeared, it was the equivalent of their church closing—so they also disappeared.

This syndrome is becoming rare as cohesive staff teams replace the superstar preacher as the glue that holds the congregation together.

10. High Expectations in the Low Commitment Church

This candidate to become the next pastor has carefully studied the record of several nationally famous megachurches and devoured the literature in the field. During the interview process, this candidate had explained to members of the search committee that, "If you call me as your next pastor, I plan to introduce this, that, and this. If you don't want to go down that road, let's terminate this process right now!" The suggested new approaches to ministry may be the development of dozens of small groups or the slogan to transform this into a tithing congregation or the challenge that every member will become an active disciple or the mandate to expand local outreach ministries or to reach large numbers of younger adults. The details do not matter. Most of the members of the search committee are (1) dazzled or (2) convinced this is the ideal prescription for this congregation or (3) tremendously impressed by the candidate's creativity, commitment, and enthusiasm or (4) persuaded that God has blessed them with the ideal candidate or (5) all of the above.

This candidate is called, arrives, and within a few months

discovers one fact the search committee had failed to mention. This is a low commitment congregation! All the action plans that the candidate described are compatible with, and emerged from, a high commitment congregational climate.

What is the appropriate next step? Transform this into a high commitment church? Should the newly arrived pastor create a long-range planning committee that will design a relatively slow-paced strategy of incremental change over the next seven to ten years? Should the new pastor seek to find happiness in a low commitment church? Should the new pastor take literally the advice of Jesus in Luke 9:5 and depart for a more promising opportunity? Or should the focus be on finding a bigger hammer to make those high expectation dreams fit a low commitment congregation?

11. The Mismatch

An increasingly common scenario finds what is essentially a good congregation served by a good pastor, but it is a bad match. One example is the highly competent, but moderately introverted minister who excels in professional skills, but is weak on interpersonal skills, who follows the long-tenured pastor who designed that congregation as a large network of one-to-one relationships with that personable, energetic, caring, extroverted, and charming minister at the hub of the network.

A second example is the minister who is an inspiring preacher, a superb teacher, a charming dinner guest, and a loving pastor. The number one need at this point in this congregation's history, however, is for a pastor who can (1) articulate a vision of a new tomorrow for that congregation, (2) design the strategy required to offset the attachment to the status quo, and (3) mobilize the resources and support required to turn the vision into reality. Instead the pastor proposes a radical change that can be defended from a rational point of view, but the vote at the congregational meeting is only fifty-two to forty-eight in support of that proposed change. With effective leadership that vote could have been ninety-six to four.

WHAT IS THE CONGREGATIONAL CULTURE?

Another half dozen common syndromes reflect the culture of that congregation. Change will be difficult unless the congregational culture is altered.

12. THE COMPLACENT CHURCH

The largest number of complacent congregations (1) average between thirty-five and sixty at worship, (2) are served by a highly competent bivocational minister or a part-time pastor, (3) meet in a comfortable and well-maintained building, and (4) enjoy a high level of internal harmony.[1]

The second largest number are those that average between 125 and 160 at worship and are served by a competent, long-tenured, and personable full-time pastor who is exceptionally happy in this role and has no desire to move.[2]

A smaller group comes from among those congregations that average between 350 and 450 at worship and enjoy the leadership of a competent, compatible, and caring staff team.[3]

Nearly everyone is comfortable with the status quo. There is a notable absence of internal discontent, bickering, griping, and backbiting. Complacency is the dominant characteristic—and there are many good reasons to support this feeling of complacency. At the top of that list is a remarkably good match between pastor (or staff) and the people.[4]

From the interventionist's perspective, the number one barrier to change is the absence of a sense of urgency[5]—and that is a central characteristic of the complacent congregation.

13. THE SUBSIDIZED CHURCH

The 1960s popularized the concept that denominational treasuries should place a high priority on subsidizing individual congregations. The four favorite recipients of these financial subsidies were (1) rural congregations, (2) new missions, (3) numerically declining inner-city parishes, and (4) ethnic minority churches.

While the Episcopal Church, the Roman Catholic Church, the

Methodist Church, the Christian Reformed Church, and the Congregational Churches had a long history of subsidizing congregations, this did not become a widely popular strategy until the 1960s. One influential factor was the growing financial subsidies granted by the federal government to farmers, homeowners, cities, public transportation systems, institutions of higher education, and the elderly. Another was the abundance of money in denominational treasuries.

In recent years the shrinking number of dollars in denominational treasuries has made it more difficult to create new subsidies. More important, however, has been the growing recognition that financial subsidies often tend to (1) create a dependency attitude, (2) encourage an adversarial relationship between the source and the recipient of that subsidy, (3) make perpetuation of the subsidy a high priority on the agenda of the recipient, (4) undermine self-esteem, local initiative, and a venturesome spirit, and (5) encourage the use of a planning model based on liabilities, weaknesses, and old images.

From a ministerial perspective, in several denominations the issue has been redefined in recent years to one of jobs for what has become a surplus of fully credentialed clergy.

Given these and other negative characteristics of financial subsidies, the interventionist may be well advised to replace that old dependency model with a new entrepreneurial model.[6] Among the best examples of that new model are literally thousands of immigrant, Afrocentric, African American, black, and charismatic Anglo churches in the large central cities.

14. The Rural Church Surrounded by Urbanites

As recently as 1950, the rural sections of North America were populated largely by rural residents. Many of them were the third or fourth generations on that family tree in that rural community. Many were served by a nearby rural church.

During the second half of the twentieth century, five trends changed that scenario, (1) millions of rural residents have moved to the cities or the suburbs, (2) approximately 30 million residents of rural North America of 1950 have died or moved into nursing homes, (3) an estimated 30,000 rural churches in the United States and Canada either closed or merged into another congregation, (4) the majority of the 75 million rural residents of North America are either retired or depend on a paycheck from an urban-type job to put food on the table, and (5) at least 10,000 new churches have been planted in rural areas to serve this new urban population living in rural communities.

These changes raise seven questions for the person working with churches in rural communities.

1. Is this a rural church displaying a rural religious subculture for rural residents?

2. Are most of the new residents in this community really urbanites who seek to combine a city paycheck with country living?

3. Which churches in the larger community have been effective in reaching, serving, and assimilating these new urbanites who live here?

4. What can be learned from their ministries?

5. Which would be the more prudent course of action, to encourage these long-established rural churches to seek to reach the new urban residents or to plant new missions to reach the new urbanites?

6. If the decision is to transform these rural churches into congregations that serve the new urbanites, what changes will be required?

7. Who will initiate those changes?

15. STAFF DISLOYALTY

Perhaps the most unpleasant of all these syndromes is the one in which the interventionist discovers that the heart of the current problem is a staff member who is undermining the ministry of the pastor.

One example is the church secretary who declares, "I am guided by three loyalties. The first is to what I believe God wants this congregation to be and to be doing. The second is what I believe will be best for this congregation. The third is my loyalty to the volunteer leaders."

Another is when a program staff member and/or the associate minister deliberately and secretly opposes the recommendations of the senior minister.

A third is when a staff member, often innocently, openly, and sincerely, attempts to compensate for the perceived limitations of the senior pastor. "The reason I am calling on you is because the senior minister likes to read and doesn't like being with people." "You must come to church next Sunday. Our pastor will be out of town and we're having a guest minister who is really a good preacher!"

Since most North American churches no longer offer the death sentence for disloyalty, the next best alternative is a resignation. Too often, however, that resignation comes from the pastor.

16. The Comfort of Growing Smaller

Many adults who have lost thirty or forty pounds of excess weight rejoice about how good they now feel.

What is more surprising to the evangelistic Christian is how comfortable a 1 or 2 or 3 percent annual decrease in the size of their congregation can be for longtime members. A common example is the congregation that gradually grew from an average worship attendance of 140 to 210 over a period of ten years. An expansion of the Sunday morning schedule from worship followed by Sunday school to worship followed by Sunday school followed by a second worship service was both a cause and a consequence of that numerical growth. The big reason, however, for that growth was an energetic, creative, goal-driven, evangelistic, competent, task-oriented, and determined pastor who came to this congregation that had been on a plateau in size for nearly two decades. That new pastor made the goal of a 3 to 4 percent annual net increase in worship attendance the top priority. That goal was achieved. Ten years of persistent effort produced a net increase of 50 percent in worship attendance. When the normal attrition rate brought the departure of twenty members, the pastor made sure that they were replaced by twenty-five to thirty new members.

That overworked and overstressed pastor chose early retirement at age sixty-three and was followed by a gregarious, personable, caring, happy, charming, low-key, highly competent, and hardworking forty-year-old minister. During the next seven years, the average worship attendance gradually dropped to 160. One reason for that decline was that this pastor placed at the top of the priority list "taking care of the people who pay the bills" (to use the words of the aging church treasurer) and placed a low priority on enlisting new members. The normal attrition rate saw the twenty departing members replaced by only fifteen to eighteen newcomers.

How did the people respond to this gradual decline in size? Most felt very comfortable. "Eliminating the early service that rarely brought out more than seventy people means we now have a full church at the regular service." "I've finally caught up with getting acquainted with people. I now feel that I know nearly everyone. Before, the place was filled with strange faces." "The new pastor is a lot more accessible. Before, you had to make an appointment to see the minister. Now I just drop in and I seldom have to wait more than a few minutes to see the pastor." "It's more like one big family now!" "The pace was too fast in the old schedule. Now we have a half hour to visit with people between Sunday school and church." "In only three years I feel I've gotten better acquainted and am closer to this minister than I was with the predecessor after ten years."

Growing smaller may not be consistent with the Great Commission, but it sure can be a source of comfort!

17. The Dysfunctional Church

The last of these seventeen syndromes is the most complicated, and the emergence of this category may be, at least in part, a product of the greater use of that word *dysfunctional.* A few years ago the president of a West Coast theological school reported that, compared to earlier classes, an increasing proportion of the new students now come from dysfunctional families or personal backgrounds.

Several of the recent presidents of the United States and many of the most highly visible political leaders in North

America were reared in what today would be defined as dysfunctional families. The Kennedy family may stand out as America's favorite dysfunctional family while the English point to the royal family as their favorite. The reason for this is clear. With but two exceptions, every family on the North American continent meets the definition of a dysfunctional household. The two exceptions, of course, are your family and my family.

At least a few observers contend that dysfunctional congregations tend to attract dysfunctional personalities as their pastors. If every institution organized around interpersonal relationships is, at least to a modest degree, a dysfunctional organization and if every adult displays at least an occasional tendency of the dysfunctional personality, that generalization obviously does reflect contemporary reality.

The issue, of course, is one of degree. In addition, the self-fulfilling expectation is a significant variable. Whether it be a parish consultant or a candidate to fill a pulpit vacancy, one often finds what one is seeking. Thus the person looking for signs of a dysfunctional institution usually will find at least a few.

After thirty-five years of consultations with hundreds of congregations, this observer has come to several conclusions on this subject of dysfunctional individuals and dysfunctional institutions.

1. This is more likely to be a serious issue for the minister being considered to fill a pulpit vacancy than it is for the parish consultant.

2. This is far more likely to be a serious issue for the professional intentional interim pastor than for the parish consultant.

3. This is far more likely to be a serious issue for the person or committee responsible for credentialing recent seminary graduates than for the parish consultant.

4. This is far more likely to be a serious concern for members of a pulpit search committee and for denominational officials responsible for ministerial placement than it is for the parish consultant.

5. This is more likely to be a serious concern for the person

seeking to reform denominational systems than it is for the parish consultant.

6. The vast majority of invitations for parish consultations originate in congregations that are relatively healthy institutions in psychological terms. Only a minority come from what clearly are dysfunctional churches.

7. A disproportionately large number of invitations for parish consultations with dysfunctional churches originate, not with the pastor or the congregational leaders, but with a frustrated denominational official seeking help. That raises a crucial question for the parish consultant. In those cases, who is the number one client? The congregation? The pastor? Or that denominational official? It is not at all uncommon for the invitation to be accompanied by an offer that the denominational agency will pay all the financial costs of that consultation.

8. From the parish consultant's perspective, one of the most frequent signs of a dysfunctional congregation is denial. One common expression of denial is the hope that next year will closely resemble 1955. Another is the conviction that everyone should walk to church. A third is that today's teenagers and younger adults should be carbon copies of people born in the 1930s. A fourth is a refusal among the leaders to recognize that the time has come to terminate the employment of a particular staff member. A fifth is that younger generations should not perceive current worship services to be dull and boring.

A common expression of denial is to replace that issue with some other means-to-an-end issue (finances, renovation of the building, acquisition of additional land, efforts to create a greater sense of unity in what is a seriously polarized congregation, relocation of the meeting place, restructuring the system of governance, creating a new staff position, and so on). Most congregational leaders are more comfortable discussing real estate or financial issues than they are with either personnel or ministry questions.

Frequently the most useful response to denial is to flood the information system with relevant information and encourage creative discussions of those data by the leaders.

HOW DOES THE INTERVENTIONIST RESPOND?

One response to the invitation to come serve as a parish consultant is to require an invitation from both the pastor and the governing board of that congregation.

A better response is to require those invitations plus full payment from the congregational treasury for all financial costs.

The best response is to accept only those invitations that originate from within the congregation that seeks your services.

The easiest, happiest, and most productive response is to avoid invitations to conduct parish consultations in what are clearly dysfunctional congregations. This kind of intervention is a long-term assignment that can be carried out more effectively by (1) the new pastor or (2) a staff person from the regional judicatory who can enter into a long-term relationship with that congregation or (3) by referring that congregation to a specialist with a high level of competence and extensive experience in working with dysfunctional organizations.

Sometime during a Christian's spiritual pilgrimage, there may come a call to become a volunteer martyr. One such opportunity may be to serve as a parish consultant to what is clearly a dysfunctional congregation. That may be part of the journey for someone who seeks to become an exceptionally wise interventionist. That may not, however, be the best road to becoming an experienced and old interventionist!

WHAT ARE THE SIGNS?

As was emphasized earlier, this subject is one of degree. What is a moderately dysfunctional congregation? What is a severely dysfunctional congregation?

Perhaps the most common sign of dysfunctionalism is the congregation founded several decades ago that has now drifted into that stage when institutional survival drives all the decision-making processes.

Overlapping that are those congregations in which taking good care of today's members, and their children, dominates the agenda to the exclusion of any expression of outreach or evangelism except for sending money to benevolent causes.

In a couple of Protestant traditions, a common expression of dysfunctionalism is when the number one criterion for both external and internal evaluation is the amount of money (1) congregations send to the denominational headquarters or (2) the amount of money a regional judicatory sends to the national headquarters of that denomination or (3) the amount of money paid the pastor in various forms of compensation. Beware when the leading volunteer lay leader boasts, "We've always paid a higher salary than any other church in town" (or in the conference or diocese or synod or district).

In larger multiple-staff congregations one of the most devastating expressions of dysfunctionalism can be seen when one or more of the professional staff redefine the role from helping that congregation to fulfill its mission and undergirding the ministry of the senior pastor to undermining and destroying the ministry of that senior pastor.

An increasingly common expression of dysfunctionalism is when either a denominational system or a congregation changes the order of priorities to placing at the top of that list the employment, compensation, and care of pastors. A frequent symptom of this pattern is to change the nomenclature so that pastors are identified as "professionals" with a "career," rather than as persons with a "call" to a "vocation."[7]

Another symptom of institutional dysfunctionalism occasionally surfaces in the congregation relocating its meeting place to a larger and more accessible site in order to reach more people. What questions dominate the agenda in that discussion? In the relatively healthy congregation, the new agenda may include these questions. What do you believe God is calling this congregation to be and to be doing in the years ahead? Who are the unchurched people that we can and should be reaching? How will this relocation effort facilitate that? How should our call to reach and serve generations not yet born influence our planning? Are we planning to relocate in order to supplement the work and ministry of other congregations? Or are we planning to relocate to ensure our own institutional survival?

In the institutionally dysfunctional congregations, the top of the local agenda is more likely to include the following questions. How large should the new worship center be in comparison with our present facilities? How much will this cost? How many members will we lose if we relocate? How will we pay for it? Can we use the old stained-glass windows in the new building? Means-to-an-end issues replace purpose questions at the top of the agenda.

At least a few readers will contend that the number one example of dysfunctionalism in a congregation can be summarized in one word. That word is *control.* In these churches, the context for planning and decisionmaking is power. Who will gain control? Who will lose power? Will the pastor be allowed "to continue to be a dictator in the running of this church"? Or will the laity control the decision-making processes? Will one family be allowed to maintain control? Will the capability to throw the biggest tantrum be the key factor in decision making? Will threats to walk out be affirmed as paths to power?

In the healthy congregation the decision-making processes are influenced by (1) obedience to the gospel, (2) a sincere search to learn the will of the Lord, (3) prayer and cooperation, (4) listening rather than screaming, (5) the call to be faithful rather than the urge to prevail, and (6) reason rather than exclusion.

In the dysfunctional church, the decision-making process often is identified as the battlefield over control. Finally, a common sign of dysfunctionalism appears when most ministry goals are designed to re-create yesterday—especially when the goal is to re-create a yesterday that never existed.

CHAPTER NINE

What Are the Central Organizing Principles?

Joe Adams and his three buddies are avid golfers. They also are active members of Trinity Church. One Tuesday evening in February, all four came to the monthly church council meeting with a request. They asked for consideration of a new summer schedule for Sunday mornings. Instead of following the traditional year-round pattern of Sunday school at nine-thirty followed by worship at eleven o'clock, they suggested that for June, July, and August the schedule would call for worship at eight o'clock followed by Sunday school at nine and a second worship service at ten.

"That would enable those of us who like to golf to get out on the course before it gets so hot," explained Joe. "In addition, we believe that adding a second service at an early hour might eliminate the traditional summer slump and the drop in church attendance." Jack Graham added, "My wife's parents live about sixty miles north of here. We could go to the early service, take the kids up to have Sunday dinner with their grandparents, and be back before the rush-hour traffic late Sunday afternoon." Dave Ferguson, a third member of Joe's quartet of golfers, argued, "This schedule would also save the church money. By moving worship up to an earlier hour, we could cut back on air conditioning costs." Bill McGuire pointed out that the proposed schedule might also be attractive to people moving in during the summer who were seeking a church that offers an early worship service.

After listening to these pleas, the person chairing the church council pointed to a sign on the wall. It read, "Our goal is to make this a better world for children." The chairperson explained to the four golfers, "Two years ago we decided that we needed to carve out a distinctive role that would distinguish us from all the other churches in town. We decided that is our distinctive calling as a Christian congregation. We measure every policy question that comes before us against that statement. If we are convinced that a particular change will make this a better world for children, we try to implement that idea. We are convinced that this is a barren and hostile world for a child to be born into. When you are prepared to explain to us how your proposed schedule will make this a better world for children, come back and we'll listen."

The budget committee at Grace Church had been asked to cut $26,000 from the proposed expenditures for the coming year. The finance committee had decided that anticipated receipts would not be sufficient to underwrite those proposed expenditures. The person chairing the budget committee pointed out to the members, "Three years ago we, as a congregation, adopted this statement as our number one goal. This sign on the wall expresses it." The sign read, "Our calling is to make believers out of nonbelievers and to transform believers into disciples of Jesus Christ."

"We need some kind of yardstick or guideline to evaluate where we can cut $26,000 from this proposed budget," continued this chairperson. "Let's begin by using that statement on the wall as our basic criterion. The cuts should come from those items that do not directly undergird that statement of our calling. Agreed?"

The personnel committee at First Church was interviewing a candidate for the vacant position of minister of music. After a half hour of conversation, one member of the committee began to read from a 3" x 5" card. "Last year the board adopted this statement. Our number one goal for the next five years will be to strengthen our ministries with parents of very young children."

As she handed the card to the candidate, she asked, "Tell us how you would help us implement that goal if you joined our staff."

What Is the Question?

During the past three or four decades, the air over the ecclesiastical landscape has been filled with words and phrases such as "mission statements," "goals," "objectives," "niche," "vision," "ministry plans," and "statements of purpose." Most of them include considerable pious language and some are filled with quotations from the Bible. Most are too broad and too inclusive to provide specific direction in the allocation of scarce resources such as time, energy, money, and space.

To be helpful, the interventionist has to push to persuade people to focus in on what is their top priority. A common response is, "We have many priorities here. It would be impossible to put only one at the top of the list." Another answer is, "That's our problem. We can't agree on priorities. The old-timers want to perpetuate yesterday. Another group wants to make missions the top priority. Others want more Bible study. Our new minister believes the top priority is to create more small groups."

Both responses translate into the same statement. We cannot plan until we agree on what we are trying to do.

At this point the interventionist may benefit by injecting some different language into the discussion. What is your central organizing purpose? In addition to doing what most churches do in the way of worship, teaching, care of the members, and maintaining the real estate, what distinguishes you from the rest of the churches in this community? What is the central core of your identity? What is that number one criterion you use to determine priorities?

The pastor may explain, "I spend three-quarters of my time doing what most ministers do, such as sermon preparation, leading worship, preaching, teaching, administration, counseling, calling on the sick, burying the dead, and visiting prospective new members. I try to reserve about a fourth of my time to focus on what we as a congregation believe is our unique role as a church. To put it in business terms, that is our special task. Three years ago we decided our special calling was a ministry with single-parent families. We've organized all our discretionary resources, including a chunk of my time and the efforts of about a dozen volunteers here, to enlarge and enrich our ministries with single-parent families. That has become our number one central organizing principle."

WHAT ARE THE CHOICES?

Others may refer to this as a specialty in ministry or as a niche or as a distinctive role. A simple definition is that this becomes the top priority in the allocation of discretionary resources. Earlier paragraphs identify four examples of a central organizing principle. A far from complete list includes these forty-three common central organizing principles.

1. Word, sacrament, and liturgy.
2. A common nationality, language, racial, or ethnic heritage.
3. A long-tenured and personable pastor who also is a respected community leader.
4. Social class.
5. A narrowly and precisely defined doctrinal statement.
6. A geographical definition of community.
7. Specific, attainable, measurable, challenging, and highly visible goals.
8. Opposition to a common enemy. (Examples include the devil, lodges, sin, denominations, the Roman Catholic Church,[1] wealth, modernity, fundamentalism, Yankees, slavery, alcoholic beverages, tobacco, war, and abortion.)
9. Converting nonbelievers.
10. Denominational loyalties. (This is more influential with adults born before 1930 than with adults born after 1955.)
11. The local reputation or the community image of a particular congregation.

12. Exceptionally attractive and meaningful preaching.
13. A common occupation. (Farming, mining, and working in the mill are three examples.)
14. A strong emphasis on world missions.
15. A focus on the power of intercessory prayer.
16. A long list of local traditions.
17. Attachment to this sacred place.
18. A long history of shared experiences.
19. Survival goals that rally people together in support of institutional survival by a heavy reliance on volunteers.
20. Contemporary Christian music, drama, and a participatory style of worship.
21. Social action goals.
22. Meaningful worship experiences.
23. An extensive network of closely knit small groups.
24. "This is where all my friends go, and we enjoy growing old together."
25. A strong network of meaningful one-to-one relationships with the pastor at the hub of that network.
26. A Christian day school.
27. A central focus on the power and the gifts of the Holy Spirit.
28. An extensive and remarkably varied seven-day-a-week program that offers something for nearly everyone.
29. A role as *the* nondenominational community church as contrasted with sectarian and denominationally related congregations.
30. Meaningful responses to people's desires to learn more about the Christian faith.
31. Healing ministries.
32. An extensive and varied ministry of music.
33. An extensive network of Sunday school classes.
34. A central focus on the Eucharist.
35. Excellent liturgical worship.
36. Attractive ministries that involve a large number of teenagers.
37. Eating together.
38. That cemetery located next to the church building.

39. A role as a landlord church housing many "outside" activities and organizations and social welfare programs.

40. Two or three interrelated family trees.

41. The metachurch model that identifies the small cells, rather than individual members, as the basic building blocks for congregational life.

42. The congregation that is an active advocate for the poor, the oppressed, the dispossessed, and the needy.

43. As a multicultural congregation, our call is to serve as a reconciling force in a culture that is fragmented by a variety of lines of demarcation based on race, social class, nationality, education, income, language, and gender.

This is *not* offered as an exhaustive list! These examples of organizing principles are *not* listed in any order of importance or value or frequency or influence. Obviously some are more defensible than others.

Others may describe some of these principles more simply as the glue that holds that collection of people together.

WHY ASK?

Why should the identification of that central organizing principle be a concern to the interventionist?

The most obvious reason is that this is an essential component of a definition of contemporary reality. For many people the status quo is the benchmark against which all proposals for change will be measured. Therefore it helps to identify the existing central organizing principles. What are the components of the status quo that can and should be undergirded? What are the components of the status quo that must be changed? Frequently if the goal is to reach new generations, the answer is that the central organizing principle must be redefined or supplemented.

One example of a redefinition of the central organizing principle is offered by a scholar who has suggested, ". . . that liberalism needs to become a counterculture to secularism, instead of a reaction to fundamentalism."[2]

Second, one of the reasons many congregations find it difficult to reach and serve new generations of people is the absence of one central organizing principle. A common example is the congregation of two or three hundred members that was founded several decades ago. For one group of older members the central organizing principle is to perpetuate yesterday into tomorrow. For another smaller group it is the loyal support of the goals of that denomination or of that regional judicatory. For a few dozen adults it is deep loyalty to their Sunday school class. For fifteen to twenty adults, the central organizing principle that generates their support is the chancel choir or the choir director. For others the number one rallying point is support for their beloved pastor. For many others the central organizing principle is this congregation meets their need for membership in an extended family where people sincerely love, care for, and support one another. For several women their number one rallying point is the women's organization and its missional goals.

The absence of a single central organizing principle makes it very difficult to design a ministry plan. Occasionally the new minister will respond to this by suggesting a new rallying point that will overshadow all those diverse organizing principles. One common example is the capital funds campaign to retire all indebtedness. A second is to construct an addition to the building or to remodel the old meeting place. These share two common limitations. First, both focus people's attention on means-to-end issues. By definition a worshiping community is not created to focus on money or real estate. Second, what happens when the capital funds campaign or the building program is completed? The usual answer is to drift in a goalless manner.

A third reason for allocating one chapter to this subject is the need for intentionality in designing a ministry plan. By definition both the individual Christian and every Christian congregation is called to live an intentional life. How can a congregation live an intentional life when there is an absence of agreement on why we exist?

SIX BASIC QUESTIONS

1. Which of these central organizing principles stand out in this congregation? Rank the four or five in order that provide much of the glue that holds this congregation together.

2. Which of those central organizing forces no longer are the powerful cohesive factors they once were in this congregation? What has replaced them? If they have not been replaced, what are the implications?

3. Has the number of these cohesive forces increased or decreased in recent years? What are the implications of those changes?

4. Is denominational loyalty a stronger or weaker cohesive force in this congregation than it was twenty years ago? Why? What are the implications of that change?

5. Which of the most influential organizing principles in this congregation reinforce and undergird other cohesive forces? Which ones appear to be divisive?

6. Which of the most influential cohesive forces on this list will tend to attract newcomers and encourage them to return? (Numbers 12, 14, 15, 22, 26, 28, 30, 36, 41, and 43 are ten common examples.) Which of the most common cohesive forces on that list may discourage first-time visitors from returning? (Numbers 2, 4, 16, 19, 24, 38, 39, and 40 are eight common examples.) Next, add at least four other cohesive forces to each of these two lists. Which of these two sets of cohesive forces (attractive or repelling) are at the top of the list of central organizing principles in this congregation?

WINNERS AND LOSERS

What are the best central organizing principles for a congregation? Which ones are at the bottom of the list? Those two questions move this discussion up from a descriptive analysis to the more subjective level of values.

It is fairly easy to build both a New Testament base and a pragmatic defense of four good central organizing principles for congregations. These are worship, teaching, evangelism, and missions.

What are the least productive organizing principles for congregations? That is a fairly easy question. First, while often it is easy to rally long-tenured members around means-to-an-end needs, these rarely are attractive when the goal is to reach new generations with the good news that Jesus Christ is Lord and Savior. Among the most widely used of these central organizing principles are (1) remodeling an old building or constructing a new one, (2) paying off debts accumulated from the past, (3) providing attractive employment opportunities for adults, (4) raising money to be sent to far-away organizations that will decide which causes eventually will receive those dollars, (5) attracting new generations to prolong the life of dying institutions, and (6) maintaining the cemetery located next to the church building.

On the positive side are an equal number of attractive and productive organizing principles for congregations, (1) gathering people together to worship and praise God, for the proper administration of the sacraments (ordinances), and the proclamation of God's Word, (2) converting nonbelievers into believers, making learners out of believers, transforming learners into disciples, and challenging disciples to be engaged in doing ministry, (3) organizing people to participate in the classical "seven corporal works of Christian mercy"—(feed the hungry, clothe the naked, shelter the homeless, care for the orphan, tend the sick, visit the prisoner, and bury the dead), (4) mobilizing the resources required for planting new congregations to reach new generations of people all over this planet, (5) creating new channels for transmitting the Christian faith to children and youth, and (6) helping to create a better environment for the rearing of children.

As the years turn into decades and time passes, internal pressures often force three organizing principles to the top of the congregational agenda. These are to take better care of (1) today's members, (2) the children of today's members, and (3) the real estate. That natural, normal, and predictable tendency of institutions to become increasingly self-centered is one of the basic arguments for planting new congregations organized around outreach. That predictable tendency also helps to explain why a higher level of competence is required of the pastor who is asked to "renew" an old established congregation than is required of the pastor who goes out to plant a new mission.

Conflicting Goals

Which is better? For a congregation to display one central organizing principle? Or to have five or six powerful central organizing principles tied for first place?

Which is better? For all the members to be in total agreement on the number one central organizing principle? Or for this group of members to lift up one while a second group insists that a different principle is central, and three or four other groups are supportive of other principles?

The answer can be summarized in two words. "It depends." If the focus is on cohesion and strengthening the sense of belonging, it may be useful to have a half dozen organizing principles tied for first place. The nationality, the heritage, reinforces the sense of belonging of this group. The emphasis on local traditions makes several dozen other members feel at home. Identifying strongly with a particular denominational heritage may help older new members affirm that this was the right choice for them. The attractive personality of the pastor is the tie that binds for another cadre. Sending twenty-five cents out of every dollar to missions reinforces the allegiance of another group of members. Placing a high priority on the maintenance of that sacred meeting place satisfies several dozen other members. In other words, if reinforcing cohesion is the number one goal, an abundance of organizing principles can be an asset.

If, however, the number one goal is (1) to raise the level of quality or (2) to enable the pastor to manage his or her time and energy more effectively or (3) to carve out a distinctive niche in a community filled with churches competing with one another for new members or (4) to design a comprehensive, internally consistent, and coherent ministry plan or (5) to maximize the benefits of an intentional interim pastorate or (6) to prepare the outline for the first few chapters in the next volume of the history of this congregation or (7) to make informed and internally consistent decisions on the allocation of scarce resources (volunteers, staff time and energy, space, money, creativity, et al.) or (8) reach new generations of people, then life will be easier and happier if there is broad-based agreement on one central organizing principle.

One source of destructive internal conflict is when the pastor and the volunteer leaders cannot agree on a single central organizing principle. Another is when serious disagreement exists between the senior minister and the program staff of the large church.

Creating that broad-based agreement may be the most valuable single contribution the interventionist can make.

CHAPTER TEN

Evangelism or Intervention?

"Our number one problem is that we can't reach the younger generations. Our members are growing older in age and fewer in number. If we don't attract more young people, our church will die. Can you come help us?" The plea is representative of many requests for the assistance of an intentional interventionist.

Frequently it comes from the pulpit search committee seeking a thirty-five-year-old pastor with forty years of experience in numerically growing churches on the assumption, "If we call a young minister, that will enable us to attract more young people." Sometimes this request is directed to a parish consultant. More often it is addressed to a specialist in evangelism or church growth or a denominational staff person.

One reason this plea is heard so often is that at least two-thirds—and perhaps as many as four-fifths—of all Protestant congregations on the North American continent founded before 1970 are either on a plateau in size or shrinking in numbers. Concurrently the total worship attendance in all Protestant churches on this continent on the typical weekend is setting a new record year after year. How does the interventionist respond to this plea?

FOUR RESPONSES

At least four responses merit discussion here.

First, the most common, and often the least helpful response is to take this plea literally and to suggest alternative church growth strategies. Occasionally this will lead to the implementation of a productive course of action.[1] Far more often, however, this will lead to frustration. The symptom, numerical decline, is not the problem. That symptom usually is a sign of one of two conditions. One is a resistance to change. The people are unwilling to make the changes necessary to reach, attract, serve, and assimilate new generations, and the leaders do not possess the skills required to initiate and effectively implement planned change from within an organization. Change often means displacement, and people naturally resist displacement.

More common is the absence of agreement on priorities, on what needs to be done to reach potential new members, and on defining the central task or core purpose of that congregation. These two conditions can be illustrated by a half dozen common patterns.

1. "We don't need off-street parking! We need to learn how to reach the people who live within walking distance of our building." The absence of off-street parking means this congregation cannot attract the people who resemble today's members, but who are a generation younger. The inability to change means that this congregation cannot reach nearby residents who come from a different nationality, racial, cultural, ethnic, generational or doctrinal slice of the population.

2. "We're a friendly congregation. We welcome strangers. We can't understand why so few first-time visitors return." One reason is that many first-time visitors, especially those born after 1955, are looking for a church that will offer meaningful responses to their religious needs. Their social needs can be satisfied elsewhere.

3. "Our minister is a wonderful person who loves everybody!" That is a valuable characteristic in the pastor of a small congregation organized primarily around implementation of the record of Jesus' two great commandments.[2] Most younger church shoppers, however, are looking for a minister who combines credibility, relevance, and meaning in biblical sermons and also excels as a communicator.

4. "We're an easygoing congregation, our members enjoy being with one another, and we don't demand a lot from people." The general pattern today is those congregations that (a) project high expectations of people, (b) act out the assumption that the power of the gospel can transform lives, and (c) are equipped to help people advance on their personal spiritual journey, are more effective in attracting younger adults than those congregations that project relatively low expectations of people.

5. "We offer a worship service organized around a presentation format with an excellent chancel choir, the traditional classical hymns, and an eighteen-minute sermon. Why don't more people come here?"

One reason is the increasing proportion of the churchgoing population who prefer a participatory approach to worship and/or contemporary Christian music and/or drama and/or a band or orchestra and/or the thirty- to fifty-minute teaching sermon that causes people to leave saying to themselves, "I'm glad I came, I learned something about the faith today that will enrich my life forever." Or, "That was an inspiring worship service!"

In other words, the central issue for these five congregations is not church growth, it is a capability to change.

6. "My problem is time," declared the pastor of a congregation founded in 1922 that peaked in size in 1955 with an average of nearly 400 at worship and now averages 135 at worship. "I spend at least seven to ten hours a week in one-to-one counseling, I preach on forty-six or forty-seven Sundays every year, I chair an important denominational committee in this conference, I am working on my doctor of ministry degree, people here still expect the pastor to call on them in their homes, I spend another twelve to fifteen hours a week in administration, I average one funeral a month, currently I am president of the local Lions Club, since I am the only staff person, I also have the basic responsibility for youth and Christian education, and I have to make all the hospital calls. If we had more staff, I believe this congregation could grow."

One alternative for this congregation is to add specialized program staff. A second is to remain on a plateau in size. A third is for that pastor, with the support of the volunteer leaders, to define narrowly, precisely, and clearly the number one task or responsibility for the next two or three years. What is the value added to that congregation's life by paying that pastor to be their minister? Unless and until that pastor's number one responsibility is clarified, the congregation will not grow. Like many physicians, university professors, public school teachers, nurses, and countless bureaucrats, this pastor is suffering from a condition called "splintered attention."[3] The solution is not to work more hours per week, but to "work smarter."

If the central goal in this congregation is numerical growth, four questions must be answered.

1. Who are the people we seek to reach and what are their needs?

2. Are we willing to make all other demands on our pastor's time secondary priorities?

3. What will our pastor not do in order to lead us in achieving our central goal?

4. Can our pastor devote at least one-fourth of every workweek to achieving that goal?

THE CANDIDATE'S RESPONSE

A second and overlapping response is offered by the candidate to fill that vacant pulpit. What does that candidate say when confronted with the question, "Do you believe you can help us reverse our numerical decline and reach more younger people?" The candidate who is eager to receive that call may reply simply, "Yes." The wise candidate will reply with a question, "Are you willing to make the changes required to accomplish that? If you are, with God's help, I believe we can do it. If you are unwilling to change, I believe I am not the person you seek."

Or the candidate may reply, "If we can agree that reaching people beyond our membership is both the number one priority of this congregation and the number one priority on my time and energy, I believe we can reverse the numerical decline of recent years. If, however, you want to make the care of today's members the number one task of this congregation and the number one call on my time, I'm afraid I'm not the person you seek."

THE STAFFER'S RESPONSE

A third response may come from the interventionist who is on the staff of the regional judicatory of that denomination. In addition to identifying the changes required to reverse that pattern of numerical decline, this interventionist may ask five additional questions. First, how can our regional judicatory resource congregations like this one most effectively? By customized parish consultations? Through in-service training experience for pastors? By specialized training events for lay volunteers? By providing new resources such as videotapes and Bible study programs? By building a mentoring relationship between a congregation that has an impressive track record in reaching younger generations and this church?

Second, is our system of ministerial placement compatible with church renewal? Third, do we need to take a new look at how we enlist, train, and apprentice the next generation of parish pastors? Fourth, are there other systemic issues in our whole denominational structure that may be causing so many of our congregations to grow older and smaller? Finally, what can our denominational systems do to enhance the quality of ministry in our congregations?

In other words, that denominational interventionist may begin with an examination of the entire system. Do the expectations projected from our denomination to our congregations "splinter" or divide their attention? Do these expectations make it difficult for the congregation to define its core purpose and to allocate the local resources in support of that core purpose? Do we project conflicting expectations of pastors that make it difficult for them to "work smarter." Do we splinter their attention? Can we help congregations redesign their organizational structure so they can make reaching the unchurched their number one priority? Or do we require the same organizational structure of all congregations? Can we help this pastor decide, "I don't do that because that is irrelevant to our central or core purpose," and not feel guilty about not doing it?

The Consultant's Response

A fourth response may be offered by the parish consultant who begins with five questions. First, why has this congregation been growing older and smaller? Second, what changes will be required to reverse that numerical decline? Third, who are the people here who are both willing and able to lead in making these changes? Fourth, what must be done here to enable this congregation to move reaching the unchurched to the top of the priority list? What must be done here to enable the pastor, or the entire program staff, to "work smarter" by concentrating their time and energy on that core purpose? Fifth, what are the most receptive points for intervention in this whole system?

This can be illustrated by looking at literally thousands of larger congregations that could and should be growing in numbers, but instead are shrinking in size. The number one reason is the absence of a widely supported strategy for reaching newcomers to that community. It matters little whether that strategy is designed around (1) inviting people to come and participate in a lively and meaningful worship experience on Sunday morning or (2) reaching potential future members through a superior seven-day-a-week teaching ministry or (3) expecting to intervene in the lives of the unchurched at strategic points in the life cycle or (4) building an attractive multicultural congregation or (5) intervening in the lives of people at strategic points on a personal spiritual journey that begins with the skeptics, doubters, and agnostics, and is designed to help people move from nonbelievers to believers to learners to disciples to apostles or (6) strengthening the two-generation family or (7) challenging believers to become involved in doing ministry locally or (8) creating a growing number of off-campus ministries or (9) creating a network of small groups.

The crucial issue is NOT the central theme of that strategy. The crucial question is whether the congregation, including the configuration of the paid staff, is organized to be supportive of a clearly defined and widely supported central strategy.

A common alternative is to perceive the congregation as a collection of interest groups. The driving goal is to keep each interest group reasonably content by assigning each one a staff person. Music has its staff person as does Christian education, youth, the mature adults, and worship. A part-time staffer is hired to call on potential future members, but that is an isolated assignment.

The primary role of the parish consultant in these settings is not to serve as a specialist in church growth, but rather as an *outside* agent of planned change. This means placing a high priority on (1) diagnosis, (2) identifying and enlisting allies in the change process, (3) designing alternative strategies for change, and (4) winning support of local "insiders" for at least one of those strategies. This also means identifying the focal point for change. In many smaller congregations this will be either helping the leaders define a new core purpose and/or encouraging the pastor to focus more narrowly on the top priority in the allocation of that minister's time and energy. In large congregations the focus may be on creating a strategy for church growth that wins broad-based support. In the large multiple-staff parish the primary focus may be on the changes necessary to move from a series of individually staffed separate empires to staffing a single strategy.

This raises a new series of questions for the interventionist. How much change can this congregation accept without being overwhelmed or immobilized or polarized?

Three Levels of Change

Change can be subdivided into three levels, each reflecting a degree of change.[4] Which level will be appropriate here?

First level changes usually are compatible with continuity with the past. This often means continuing to do what we have been doing, only better. The primary focus is on quality. This may mean improving the existing in-service training program for teachers or better quality communication with first-time visitors or a 30 percent increase in the size of the parking lot or improving the quality of the bulletin for Sunday morning worship or adding a page describing future events and programs.

Other first level changes may involve (1) videotaping the Sunday morning worship service and evaluating it on Thursday evening before choir rehearsal or (2) remodeling the building to create a more attractive entrance or (3) recruiting a few more good voices for the choir or (4) improving the system for following up on first-time visitors or (5) air-conditioning the worship center or (6) encouraging the preacher to take instruction on effective communication in an electronic era.[5]

Intervention with first level changes often is compatible with the goal of raising the rate of increase in worship attendance from an annual average of 2 percent to an annual average of 3 percent or even 4 percent. Keep on doing what you are doing, only do it better.

If, however, the goal is to reverse a long period of numerical decline, this usually will require second or third level changes. Second level changes are modest in scale and often are accomplished by a system of incremental change. A common example is to add a second (or third) and substantially different worship experience to the weekend schedule to reach people who will not attend "the regular service." Another is to add one new adult class to the Sunday school every year. A third example is to build a network of small groups that eventually will include as regular active participants 20 to 40 percent of all adults. A fourth is to create a variety of additional entry points for newcomers by (1) adding one or two more services to the Christmas Eve schedule or (2) adding another weeklong session of vacation Bible school or (3) creating one or two new mutual support groups annually or (4) organizing a new high school youth group for the teenagers who will not participate in the current program or (5) extending the current weekday nursery school to include kindergarten or (6) increasing the level of member contributions by 15 percent.

Ideally this system of "change by addition" will not disrupt the ongoing life of the current program or schedule.

For many numerically shrinking congregations (and denominational systems) the best that can be expected of second level changes will be to slow, or possibly halt, the rate of decline. If the goal is to move from growing older and smaller to growing younger and larger, this usually will require third level changes. These are often identified, especially by those who value the status quo, as radical changes. They do represent a radical departure from the status quo. Examples include (1) relocating the meeting place, (2) replacing traditional church music with contemporary Christian music, (3) urging the current pastor to resign or take early retirement, (4) completely redesigning the Sunday morning schedule, (5) dropping the traditional approach to Christian education and building a learning community or (6) replacing the traditional emphasis on sending money away for missions to challenging volunteers to be engaged in doing missions.

For most smaller congregations the proposal to place reaching the unchurched ahead of taking care of today's members is perceived as radical change. For many large multiple-staff parishes a proposal to replace individualized assignments for paid program staff members with a central strategy supported by staff teams represents radical change. For many pastors of middle-sized congregations, the idea of concentrating on a single task rather than living with splintered attention is somewhere between radical change and utopian thinking!

One of the crucial questions for the parish consultant is what level of change should be recommended here? First level? Second level? Third level?

The next question for the interventionist concerns the points of intervention.

Personal Intervention

The first point of intervention usually is in the life, culture, ministry, and systems of that congregation. The second is where will this parish seek to intervene in the lives of people who are not actively involved in the ministry of any church? How do we invite them to come to our church?

1. A common point of intervention is to send unsolicited messages to people inviting them to participate in what we offer. This can be accomplished via newspaper advertisements, the Yellow Pages, direct mail, door-to-door calling, flyers hung on doorknobs, radio, television, and other channels. The recipients may be invited to attend worship, send their children to our vacation Bible school, come to our Christmas Eve services, help to pioneer a new adult class in the Sunday school or any one of many other events, activities, programs, services, or ministries we offer or plan to create.

2. A powerful type of intervention is the personal witness. Members live out the popular song, "They'll know we are

Christians by our love." Volunteers work in nursing homes, call on the shut-ins, feed the hungry, shelter the homeless, visit those in prison, care for needy children, crusade for world peace, assist in the hospice for the terminally ill, and other acts of Christian mercy.

3. Instead of inviting people to come to our church, we go to them. These congregations concentrate on reaching the unchurched on neutral turf. Volunteers organize a variety of "off-campus" ministries in storefronts, nursing homes, college dormitories, large apartment buildings, mobile home courts, vacation centers, or new sites. The goal is to meet people on their turf.

4. A productive alternative is to intervene at strategic points in the life cycle. Common examples include: (a) the weekend retreat for newly engaged couples, (b) the new Sunday school class for newlyweds in their first marriage, (c) the parenting class for people anticipating the arrival of their first child, (d) marriage enrichment events, (e) the class for parents of newborn babies, (f) the weekday nursery school, (g) the Christian day school, (h) the mutual support group for those in the process of divorce, (i) the new adult Bible study–prayer group for newlyweds in their second or subsequent marriage (out of 2.4 million weddings in the United States in 1993, in 54 percent this was the first marriage for both the bride and groom, in 23 percent it was the first marriage for one and the second or subsequent marriage for the other, and in 23 percent both had been married previously), (j) the mutual support group for parents living with a teenager for the first time, (k) the new adult class for empty nest couples, and (l) the mutual support group for the recently widowed.

5. In recent years the most rapidly expanding expression of intervention is with adults on a self-identified personal spiritual quest. A common beginning point is one Sunday morning service designed to present the truth and relevance of the gospel to doubters, skeptics, agnostics, searchers, seekers, pilgrims, explorers, and other inquirers. Typically this experience includes persuasive preaching (apologetics), drama, and contemporary Christian music.

This beginning point is supplemented with (1) one or more worship experiences designed for believers, (2) an array of learning opportunities for new believers who want to learn more about the Christian faith in general and the Bible in particular, (3) challenges for these learners to become disciples (to advance from admirers of Jesus to become followers of the Christ) through a discipling program, (4) training experiences for volunteers in ministry, and (5) carefully designed opportunities to be engaged in doing ministry.

Given the culture, resources, strengths, potentialities, leadership, and place on the theological spectrum of that particular congregation, the parish consultant asks five questions: (1) What is the appropriate method for this congregation to intervene in the lives of the unchurched and/or the pilgrimages of today's church shoppers? (2) What will be the most effective strategy for making that a meaningful intervention? (3) What changes will be necessary to enable this congregation to implement that strategy of intervention? (4) Who are the local allies who can initiate and implement those required changes? and (5) What additional resources will be needed to implement that strategy and what are the potential sources of those resources?

One expression of evangelism is to plant new missions. A second is to hold revivals and rallies. A third is to intervene in the ongoing life and ministry of three-quarters of the long-established congregations on the North American continent.

CHAPTER ELEVEN

393 Diagnostic Questions

The heart of the methodology suggested in this book is questions. Earlier chapters have included dozens of questions that can be asked by interventionists. This chapter expands on that theme.

What are the questions the interventionist should ask? One answer is, "Lots!" A better response is to back off and look at several major categories of diagnostic questions. One group, here called advance preparation questions, is asked before arrival on the scene. A second group consists of the questions evoked by a visual examination after arrival. The third and largest group consists of what I call the starter questions. These are designed to be asked early in the interview process. An overlapping fourth group consists of the "Where Am I?" questions introduced in previous chapters. The last category consists of the questions evoked by the responses to earlier questions.

That third category of starter questions requires a further word of explanation. These questions are designed to evoke responses that will stimulate the asking of additional questions. The generic label for one group of these follow-up questions can be condensed into two words—"How come?" (See chapter 3.) A longer version is, "Tell me why you said that." In real life those questions usually are customized to match the response to the starter question. For example, several years ago I was meeting with a group of high school juniors and seniors who had part-time jobs during the school year and full-time employment during the summer. One of my starter questions was, "What are you saving your money for? How will you use your accumulated savings?" (Occasionally with some teenagers born in the 1969–83 era, I have had to define the word *savings*.) In this parish the second person to respond was a sixteen-year-old high school junior. Her seven-word reply was, "I'm saving up to buy a truck." My "How come?" question was stated in only six words, "Why don't you buy a car?" Her five-word answer was, "I already have a car."

On a Tuesday afternoon I asked a pastor's wife my last starter question, "What should I have asked you to help me better understand this situation but I didn't know enough to ask that question?" She replied, "You should have asked me when I am going to move. The answer is Saturday. In four days I'm leaving my husband and moving into my own apartment."

This introduces those follow-up questions that carry the generic label, "Tell me more." I asked, "If you don't mind, please tell me more. I think I need a better understanding of what's going on here." She explained, "This past weekend we took our youngest child, our seventeen-year-old daughter, off to college. Now that she's gone, I don't have to put up with this SOB anymore."

In a Presbyterian church I asked that same starter question of a man who was reputed to be one of the most widely respected and influential leaders in that congregation. He said, "You should have asked about the plans my wife and I and a few of our friends have." So, I inquired, "Tell me about those plans." He explained in a voice filled with a combination of excitement, anticipation, and regret, "Next month the associate pastor and about forty of us are leaving here to start a new nondenominational church."

I interrupted, "How many people around here know about this?" He replied, "As far as I know, you're the first person outside our group to know, so please keep it secret." (This immediately raised the distinction between confidentiality and anonymity identified as item 11 in chapter 2.) So, I asked the tell-me-more questions about (1) why they were leaving, (2) why start a new independent church, and (3) why keep it secret?

Another category of follow-up questions can be expressed generically in nine words, "What do you want me to do about that?" Many years ago my first interview in a Pennsylvania parish was with the full-time choir director–organist. As we reached the end of our hour, I asked my "What should I have asked" starter question. He told me I should have asked if he was gay, then declared that he was gay, and said that I should know that. At that point I asked, "Does the senior pastor know this?" With considerable hesitation, he replied, "I don't know. I hope he does, but I don't think he knows." So I asked, "What do you want me to do?" He replied, "If the opportunity presents itself, I wish you would tell him. I think it would be better if he knew." (This introduces the role of the interventionist as involuntary messenger.)

My third appointment that morning was with a psychiatrist who also was an influential congregational leader. When I asked my last starter question, he explained, "You should know that the choir director–organist is gay." I challenged him, "How do you know that?"

He casually explained, "I'm one of at least a dozen people here who know that, so I'm not breaking any confidences. You need to know it, so if anyone springs it on you, you can be prepared with how you want to respond."

At noon the pastor and I met face-to-face for the first time as we went to a nearby diner for a quick lunch. After we had ordered, he asked, "Well, what have you learned this morning that I don't know but that I ought to know?" I answered, "Well, for one thing, I know your organist is gay." After he pulled himself up off the floor and climbed back onto the stool at the lunch counter, he demanded, "What makes you say that?" I shrugged and explained, "He told me he's gay and I believe him. I also believe you, as the senior minister, should know it, so that's why I'm telling you."

The last category of follow-up questions is the most difficult. These must be customized carefully and precisely to the response evoked by the previous question.

One very large congregation was served by an exceptionally competent pastor who retired after twenty-five years. The equally competent successor, the Reverend Philip Green, served for twenty-two years. An intentional, nonresident, and incompetent interim pastor followed Green, served for ten months, and was followed by a called and installed minister who turned out to be an unintentional interim pastor and resigned after twenty-six months. When I arrived, the "new pastor" was midway through the tenth year of what were clearly the best years in the eighty-year history of that congregation.

The first person on my interview schedule was a seventy-year-old widely respected former leader who had joined fifty years earlier. Eventually I asked my starter question about what distinguishes this congregation from all the other churches in town.

With no hesitation this veteran member explained, "That's easy! I've been a member here for fifty years and we have enjoyed the leadership of three consecutive pastors who are among the truly outstanding clergymen in this whole denomination. I doubt if there is another church in the whole state that's benefited from sixty consecutive years of such exceptional ministerial leadership!"

At this point I demurred by asking, "I didn't realize this was three consecutive pastorates of superb ministers. I thought you had one or two other pastors between Reverend Green and your present senior minister. Is that correct?" My objection evoked a short question, "When did you arrive in town?" I replied, "Last night."

"Well, I've been a member here for slightly more than fifty years, and I suspect I know more about this church than you do."

I persisted and finally this old-timer conceded, "Well, maybe I'm wrong. Now that you mention it, I believe we did have a supply preacher or a visiting minister who filled the pulpit for a few months after Reverend Green left to take a job in a national church agency, but I'm sure he never moved into the parsonage. Except for those few months, the present senior minister's immediate predecessor was Reverend Green!"

This conversation introduces the final category of follow-up questions. The generic label is, "What is reality here?"

In another congregation the advance preparation reported (1) the third pastorate lasted from 1965 to 1988, (2) an average worship attendance that ranged between 600 and 700 for 1972 through 1988, (3) an average worship attendance of 363 for 1989, 394 for 1990, 464 for 1991, 535 for 1992, 560 for 1993, 575 for 1994, and 688 for 1995. When I arrived, I discovered what I considered to be three significant facts, (1) the Sunday morning schedule had been expanded in September 1990 to include, for the first time in this congregation's history, two worship services, (2) a printed brochure from the dedication of the present building in 1967 that quoted the architect as stating the seating capacity for worship was 536 including the choir loft, and (3) the oral tradition that declared that the worship center was "comfortably full" with 450, but on a few occasions including a few Easters and one funeral, they had packed in nearly 500 people.

The advance preparation alleged that for sixteen years, this congregation *averaged over* 600 in worship in a room that could accommodate about 500. What is reality?

One beginning point for defining reality is the advance preparation, but that should be seen as only the first in a long process of asking questions.

1. The Advance Preparation

Before looking at these starter and other questions, however, a better beginning point consists of the questions that are included in the advance preparation. These questions can be divided into five categories and usually this is done by mail.

A. Response to an Inquiry

The process begins when someone representing that congregation inquires about the possibility of a parish consultation. This may be done in face-to-face conversation, by telephone, or by mail. As soon as possible, I try to shift it to a written format, and these are among the most common opening questions.

1. What is the agenda you want me to address?
2. How urgent is this?
3. How much time will you need?
4. What is your average worship attendance?
5. When did the present pastor arrive?
6. When was the congregation founded?
7. What is your denominational affiliation?
8. We require an official invitation from the governing board. Can you provide that?

9. We require an invitation from the pastor? Can you provide that?

10. How much land do you own?

11. Who will pay the cost of the consultation?

12. We require considerable advance preparation. Can you do that in the time available?

Subsequently, if the invitations are forthcoming and if we can agree on a date, we move to a request for additional advance preparation.

B. What issues or questions are facing this congregation?

Could I get a paragraph each from the pastor and a dozen other persons on the most urgent or important issues before this congregation today? This should be completed as soon as possible.

C. Could a planning committee or similar group respond to these questions?

It is much more helpful if this is NOT done by paid staff members!

1. Do you perceive yourself as a: ___(a) large congregation ___(b) middle-sized congregation ___(c) small congregation?

2. Do you believe your greatest era in ministry as a congregation was: __1920–40 __1940–60 __1960–80 __1980–90 __after 1990?

3. What do you, as a congregation, do best in ministry? List one program or ministry.

4. In two or three sentences, describe the most important "good" thing that has happened in or to this congregation since 1975.

5. What was the average attendance at Sunday morning worship for each of the past fifteen years?

6. What was the total membership figure reported for each of the past fifteen years?

7. What has been the average attendance at Sunday church school on a year-by-year basis from 1960 to date?

8. What is the estimated age mix of today's baptized members?

Ages 0–13___ 14–17___ 18–21___ 22–24___ 25–34___ 35–44___

45–54___ 55–64___ 65–74___ 75+___

9. The number of *resident* adult (age 18 and over) members* in each of these categories: (Count people, not couples or families, and use current marital status.)

___Husbands and wives living together with children under eighteen at home.

___Husbands and wives living togther *without children* under eighteen at home.

___Single, never-married adults.

___Currently divorced men.

___Currently divorced women.

___Currently separated from spouse.

___Currently widowed men.

___Currently widowed women.

___Total resident adult members age eighteen and over.

*If one spouse is a member and the other is not a member of your congregation, count the member in the appropriate category.

10. How many persons transferred in by letter for each of the past dozen years? How many members transferred out?

11. How many new members were received by confirmation (or profession of faith) for each of the past dozen years?

12. Complete this table showing when each of today's confirmed members joined *this* congregation.

Today's Confirmed Members	*Active*	*Inactive*	*Total*
___Joined before 1950			
___Joined 1950–59			
___Joined 1960–69			
___Joined 1970–79			
___Joined 1980–89			
___Joined 1990 to date			

13. The date (approximate) that marks the break between the newest half and the oldest half of the membership. In other words, one-half of today's confirmed members joined since that halfway mark back there and one-half joined before that date. What is that date?

14. How many *member* deaths for each of the past ten years?

15. How many child and infant baptisms (or dedications) for each of the past ten years?

16. What were the *total* receipts of this congregation for each year for the past fifteen years?

17. What were the current receipts from *member giving* for each year for the past fifteen years? (Deduct endowment income, rents, service fees, and so forth from response to question sixteen above.)

18. What was the total number of "giving units of record" for this last fiscal year?

19. The total receipts from the ten largest "giving units of record" for this last fiscal year? From the next ten largest giving units?

20. Please send a copy of last year's financial statement and this year's budget.

21. Identify the postal zip code areas that account for 90 percent of your resident member households and report how many member households live in each local zip code. (Note to reader: A large regional congregation usually reports at least thirty households in each of twenty or more zip codes.)

22. What is the pastor's home zip code?

23. What is the zip code for this church?

24. Names and dates of pastors and associate pastors who have served this congregation since 1940.

25. Does this congregation have (a) an endowment, (b) significant cash surplus, (c) any indebtedness? If yes, how much?

26. Has there been a major event or episode or change since 1940 that is still seen as a "watershed" in this congregation's history or pilgrimage?

D. The Attendance Survey

For many congregations the largest part of the advance preparation is the attendance survey covering four *consecutive*

Sundays or weekends. We suggest that to get a COMPLETE tabulation (1) give *each* worshiper (including three-year-olds) a 3" x 5" card to fill out *each* Sunday, (2) allow time during the worship service for this to be done, and (3) *give each usher a whip to make sure each attender* fills out and turns in a card *each Sunday*! It may help to use a different color card for each Sunday. After four weeks of cards have been collected, they should be tabulated either by computer or by hand.

All we need is this tabulation. Please do NOT send us the cards!

The Tabulation

	Joined before *1985**	Joined 1985 *or later**	Total
1. Members attending one Sunday			
2. Members attending two Sundays			
3. Members attending three Sundays			
4. Members attending four Sundays			
5. Average number of constituents (nonmembers)			
6. Average number of visitors			
7. Average number of children			
8. Usher count of attendance for each of these four Sundays			
9. Number of males attending three or four Sundays			
10. Number of females attending three or four Sundays			
11. Number of males attending once or twice			
12. Number of females attending once or twice			

*The date should be the same as the median tenure on question 13 of the advance preparation. The following is a suggestion for attendance survey cards:

Name____

Check one: Member___ Constituent (Nonmember)____
Child____ Visitor____

Check one: Female____ Male____

If a member, check one: Joined before 1985*____
Joined 1985* or later____

How far do you live from church? (check one):
___ 0–1 mile ___1–2 miles ___2–5 miles ___5+ miles

We ask only for a tabulation of the results of that survey. If it is appropriate, we also suggest that the 3" x 5" card include a question on the distance the respondent lives from church.

Ideally we receive this tabulation at least two months before the scheduled parish consultation.

E. Responding to the Advance Preparation

After the first round of the advance preparation has been received, this usually generates a new round of questions. Three common examples are these follow-up questions.

1. The survey of worship attendance indicates sixty members attended once during this four-week period, 60 attended twice, 70 attended three times, and 80 attended four Sundays. That produces an average worship attendance by members of 178 (60 x 1= 60 + 60 x 2 = 120 + 70 x 3 = 210 + 80 x 4 = 320 for a total of 710 ÷ 4 = 178) plus an average attendance of 7 constituents, 10 visitors, and 40 children for a grand total average of 235. The usher count ranged from 203 to 217 and averaged 209. What is the reason for that discrepancy?

2. You report 71 percent of your members joined before 1990, but give 1991 (question thirteen) as the median date of tenure for members. Which reflects reality?

3. You report a net loss of sixty-nine members over the past

seven years, but your gains and losses add up to a net loss of 107 over the past seven years. Which reflects reality?

F. Customized Questions

The information received in the first round of the advance preparation often provides the foundation for additional detailed questions.

1. Please send a roster of all persons on the payroll including name, title, year of birth, year joined staff, ordination status, whether part-time or full-time, and marital status.
2. Send the names and titles of the five most influential volunteer officers.
3. If available, please loan us a history of your congregation.
4. When did you move to your present location?
5. Do you provide church-owned housing or a housing allowance for the pastor?
6. What is the seating capacity of your worship center?
7. Does a former pastor live in your community?
8. What is the name of the largest nearby congregation of your denomination?

These and similar questions can provide useful material for preparing suggestions for an interview schedule.

2. Visual Observations

Immediately on arrrival, like any other first-time visitor, the interventionist will begin to take a visual inventory of that unique setting. What do you look for on arrival?

1. If flying in, who meets the plane? Why?
2. Who prepared the interview schedule? Why?
3. How well concealed is the church property? How difficult would it be for a stranger to find it?
4. Is it obvious what the "right" door is to enter? On Sunday morning? On Tuesday? On a rainy Thursday evening?
5. What is available for off-street parking?
6. What is the general condition of the real estate?
7. What is the appearance of the nursery? Is it near an exit on the first floor?

8. What is the appearance of the most frequently used women's rest room?

9. What is the condition of the worship center?

10. How attractive is the best large meeting room?

11. What do the corridors say to a first-time visitor?

12. What does the sign out front say to the driver of a passing motor vehicle?

13. Is the building easily accessible to the elderly and the physically impaired?

14. What does the appearance of the community context suggest?

15. How much land is available for expansion?

16. If this is a multiple-staff congregation, what does the location of the offices suggest is the configuration of staff relationships?

17. Do the members of the office staff enjoy a productive work environment?

18. How easy would it be for a first-time visitor to find the worship center? A rest room? A place to hang a topcoat? A designated meeting room?

19. What are the visible signs of a strong missional emphasis that greet the first-time visitor?

20. How many off-street parking spaces are designated as reserved for (a) mothers of young chidren, (b) visitors, (c) the physically impaired, (d) staff?

21. What is the ratio of the average worship attendance to the seating capacity of the worship center?

22. What is the message the bulletin boards send to the first-time visitor?

23. Who are depicted by the photographs on the walls? Previous pastors? Members of the governing board and other current officers? Current mission projects? Recent new members? Children? The current staff?

24. Does a different congregation meet in a building on this campus every week? If yes, what is the relationship to this congregation?

25. Does another congregation meet in this building? If yes, when? Who?

3. Starter Questions

This methodology calls for the interventionist to come with a large mental inventory of starter questions. These are useful questions for the first stage of an interview. Frequently the first few questions are simple, objective, and noncontroversial. They are framed to build rapport, to gain information, and to offer the interviewee easy answers. These starter questions can be classified by the role, office, or position of the individual being interviewed. (The reader should note that the printed word is a radically different form of communication from the spoken word. Therefore the oral wording of many of these questions will not be identical with the words printed here. Fifteen words may be appropriate in oral communication when ten words are sufficient in the printed form.)

A. General Starter Questions to Ask Pastors, Paid Staff Members, Volunteer Leaders, and Knowledgeable Individuals

1. Are you a native of this state?
2. If not, what brought you here?
3. How long have you been part of this congregation?
4. What made you choose this church?
5. Have you always been a member of this denomination?
6. Lest there be any misunderstanding, do you have any questions about who I am or why I was invited to come here or why you were asked to come in and talk with me?
7. What year were you born?
8. What is the unique or distinctive characteristic that distinguishes this congregation from all the churches in this community? We're not talking about your denominational affiliation. We're talking about your distinctive local identity or role or ministry. Tell me about that.
9. What do you see as the most pressing issue or concern on the current agenda of this congregation?
10. What do you believe is the number one strength or asset here? Brag to me for a minute about this congregation.
11. If you could wave your magic wand and cause one change to occur here, what would it be? What do you see as a highly desirable change?

12. What is the most significant change that has happened here since you became a member?

13. Picture in your mind what you would like this congregation to look like five years from now. How does that picture differ from today's reality?

14. What is the biggest barrier to making your vision become the reality of tomorrow?

15. Picture in your mind your five closest personal friends. How many of them are members of this congregation today?

16. You wanted something good to happen here, but recently you gave up on that ever happening. Yesterday, however, you learned two or three influential leaders now are determined that will happen. Given their support you now have hope that will happen. What are the names of those two or three influential leaders here?

17. Let's shift to a different perspective. Recently you became alarmed when someone came up with what you saw as a very bad idea. To your dismay it appeared this dumb idea had gained widespread support and probably would be implemented. Subsequently you discoverd two or three key members are categorically opposed to it. You relax because you know that if they oppose it, it will never be implemented. What are their names?

18. Tell me, what does your pastor do best? Brag to me about your pastor.

19. If this congregation closed tomorrow, do you now know where you probably would go for your new church home?

20. Have you noticed any of your friends who were members here have left to attend another church in this community? If yes, why did they leave?

21. Who is the most valuable player on your volunteer team here?

22. Who is the most valuable player among your paid staff?

23. How has this congregation nourished your own personal spiritual journey?

24. Finally, what's the question that I should have asked because your response would have helped me better understand this congregation, but I didn't know enough to ask that

question? Tell me what I should have asked and your response to that question.

B. Questions for the Pastor or Senior Minister

In addition to several of the starter questions from the above list, here are customized questions to ask the pastor.

1. What led you to agree to become the pastor of this congregation?
2. What reservations did you originally have about this assignment?
3. In terms of the match between you and this parish, is this today a better match than you expected it to be? Or a less favorable match?
4. What were you doing before coming here?
5. When were you ordained? In this denomination?
6. Tell me about your journey from high school to here.
7. Were you ever employed full-time in a secular job?
8. If you were to do it over again, would you follow the same educational path?
9. In terms of the family constellation into which you were born, are you a first born, a middle born, or a last born child to your mother?
10. How many siblings do you have? What are they doing?
11. Are you married? Year? Children?
12. Is your spouse employed outside the home?
13. How's your health?
14. What was your father's occupation?
15. How far from the church property is your place of residence?
16. What are your favorite reading resources?
17. What are the three areas of ministry in which you excel? What do you do best? Brag to me.
18. What does this congregation do best in ministry? Brag to me about this church.
19. What is the seating capacity here for worship?
20. What is your total compensation package here?
21. What's the best thing that has happened since your arrival?

22. What's your number one wish or dream or hope for the future here?

23. Who among the current members here is your closest personal friend?

24. Where do you expect or hope to be five years hence?

25. Are you happy here?

26. Tell me about your predecessor(s).

27. Do you know your typology on the Myers-Briggs Inventory?

28. Why was I invited to come here?

29. Who initiated that invitation? Why?

30. What is the number one agenda item you want to be sure I address?

31. Is there an especially sensitive area I should be warned about in advance?

32. Do you hope to continue as a parish pastor until you retire?

33. What is the schedule for the weekend for worship, education, and so forth?

34. If you could live your life over, would you be a parish pastor?

35. What was your attendance last Easter? How does that compare with July and August?

36. Who among the volunteer leaders are your key allies? Name five or six.

37. Among the parish pastors in this community, who are your two or three closest personal friends?

38. What is your point of greatest frustration here?

39. How active are you as a volunteer in your denomination?

40. Have you ever been a member of a different religious tradition? If yes, why did you leave it?

C. Questions for the Pastor's Spouse

If the spouse is interested and available, these may be asked in addition to several from subsection A above.

1. Where were you reared?
2. Tell me about your family constellation.
3. Are you employed outside the home?

4. What year were you born?
5. What does your spouse do best in ministry?
6. Were you reared in this religious tradition?
7. Do you know your type in the Myers-Briggs Inventory?
8. Where would you like to be five years from now?
9. Are you happy being married to a parish pastor?
10. Are you happy living in this community?
11. Are you comfortable with your housing?
12. What is the issue that you want to be sure I address during my visit?
13. What does this congregation do best in ministry?
14. Are you involved as a volunteer in this congregation?
15. Visualize in your mind the faces of your five closest personal friends. How many are members of this congregation? How many live in this community?

D. Questions for High School Students

This usually is a group interview with between five and forty high school students—most or all of whom are active in the high school youth group in that congregation.

1. Let's go around the circle and tell me your name, grade, and one thing this church does best for your age group.

2. In today's high school world, it is common for students to refer to others by a label or identity other than age or grade. Adults tend to divide the high school population into groups by age and grade. Kids like you often use other classification systems. Rarely do I hear kids like you refer to sophomores or juniors. Far more often I hear words and phrases such as jocks, treehuggers, nerds, druggies, chimneys, preppies, rednecks, kickers, the leather jacket crowd, losers, swimmers, students, and parallel parkers. What are the names that are applied to the various tribes or groups or cliques in your school?

3. How many of you own a motor vehicle that is registered in your name? (In 1995 that figure was 32 percent for teenagers with driver's licenses, up from 7 percent in 1960.) Let's see a show of hands.

4. How many of you are employed on at least a part-time basis during the school year?

5. For those with part-time jobs, what is your most meaningful form of self-evaluation? We all like to know how we're doing. We need feedback from others. Which provides the most meaningful feedback to you? Your report card? Or your paycheck?

6. For this next question we're going to divide your world into two parts. One is school. The other is the rest of your life. Let's begin with school. Where or in whom in the high school you attend do you find the greatest emphasis on quality?

7. Now, let's move to the rest of your world that includes home, church, job, hobbies, recreation, and so forth. Where in that world do you find the greatest emphasis on quality?

8. Let's pretend that this church is about to undertake a huge building program. One part of the design calls for a large second floor youth room. You will be able to have an influential voice in the design of that room, including the decorations and furnishings. At the last minute, someone suggests not doing that, but instead proposes to purchase a secondhand, reconditioned Greyhound-type bus. This would be the youth room. The first idea assumes a building-centered approach to youth ministries. The second assumes the youth program here would be organized largely around events and trips. We will take a few minutes to discuss these two alternatives. After that, you will write one word on a piece of paper to express your preference. Write either *bus* or *room* on that piece of paper and give me your preference.

9. Brag to me about the best components of the total ministry with youth in this church. What do you like best about the whole program?

10. Let's list a dozen or more places where youth can be involved in the life and ministry of this congregation on this sheet of newsprint. Which two places would be the easiest for you to cancel out completely? You may pick two off this list. We will go down the list; raise your hand when we come to one of the two you would be willing to see taken off the list. Now we will follow the same procedure to determine the two that must be kept.

11. Tell me about the role of adults, either paid staff or volunteers, in the youth ministry here.

12. What gatherings bring your big crowds? The small crowds?

13. If you could add, subtract, or change one thing about the whole youth ministry, what would you change?

14. As you talk with other kids in your school, which church appears to have the outstanding youth program in this community?

15. What is the proportion of twelfth graders compared to tenth graders who are active in the youth program here?

16. What is the typical attendance at regular meetings compared to special events?

17. Raise your hand if you have ever been president of an organization—either in school or in the larger community.

E. Questions For Volunteer Youth Staff

In addition to a few of the questions from subsection A, these may be asked.

1. Who enlisted you?
2. Why did you agree to work with youth?
3. What is your biggest personal gift in working with youth?
4. What is the basic approach or philosophy for youth ministries here? What do you seek to accomplish?
5. Who are the one or two key volunteers here? Why are they so valuable?
6. What is the role of the pastor or other paid staff in working with youth?
7. What is the typical attendance at a regular weekly meeting? At special events or retreats or trips?
8. Why do the regulars attend? What motivates them to come? Why do other youth stay away?
9. What is your number one competitor for the attention, time, and involvement of the youth?
10. How does the youth program relate to the Sunday school? To the ministry of music?
11. Where and how are youth encouraged to participate across generational lines?
12. How many high schools do you draw youth from on a regular basis?

13. How does the youth program here relate to post–high school ministries here?

14. What distinguishes the high school youth group from the junior (middle) school youth program?

15. Who are the key leaders among the youth? What grade are they in at school?

F. Paid Youth Staff

In adition to questions listed earlier, these may be asked of paid youth staff.

1. What brought you here?

2. What is your background or training in youth ministries?

3. Do you see your primary focus as on youth or on families that include teenagers?

4. What is your philosophy or basic approach to youth ministries? What do you expect to accomplish?

5. Tell me about your academic training in family systems theory.

6. Do you (a) work directly with youth or (b) enlist, train, and support adult volunteers who are the "hands on" leaders or (c) identify, enlist, train, place, and support teenagers who serve as peer leaders or (d) some combination of those approaches.

7. Who are your key staff allies?

8. Who are your key volunteer allies?

9. What is the system of accountability for the youth ministry here?

10. What is the total budget, including your compensation, or the appropriate share of your compensation, for youth ministries?

11. What is the big event or trip of the year for youth?

12. What is the role you have designed for fathers of teenagers in the youth ministry?

13. What year were you born?

14. What do you hope to be doing ten years from now?

15. How are youth here involved in intergenerational programming?

16. Do you have a system here for developing the leadership gifts of the youth?

17. What is the process or method you use for helping youth progress on their own individual spiritual pilgrimage?

G. Members of the Governing Board

1. How large is the board?
2. How often do you meet?
3. Do you have an executive committee?
4. What is the number one responsibility of your board?
5. How does the pastor relate to the board?
6. What is your current number one concern or problem or worry?
7. Who worries about money here?
8. Who oversees the real estate?
9. Who oversees program planning?
10. Who is designing the life and ministry for this congregation five years from now?
11. Who runs this church? The board? The pastor? The staff? Committees? Tradition and local precedents? Financial limitations? A widely shared vision of what God is calling us to be and to be doing?
12. What are the big differences between this congregation today and what it was five years ago?
13. Who initiated the invitation for me to come here?
14. Why?
15. What do you want to be sure we address before I leave?
16. Tell me about the staff and the staff relationships here.
17. What does your pastor do best?
18. What is the distinctive identity or role of this congregation in this community?
19. Why would new residents come here for the first time? Why would they return?
20. What is the name of the church that is your number one competitor for new residents as new members?
21. Do you believe your board would be more effective if it were larger? Or smaller?
22. What are the criteria for selecting members of the governing board?
23. Should those criteria be changed?

24. How many of the current members of the board joined this congregation during the past three years?

25. What is the weakest area of ministry here?

H. Paid Staff Members

After ten to twenty minutes with other starter questions, I may ask several of these:

1. What are your responsibilities and duties?
2. How has that changed since you joined this staff?
3. Who invited you to join the staff here?
4. Are you part-time or full-time?
5. Who is your closest personal friend on the staff?
6. Who is closest to you professionally?
7. Describe the nature of staff relationships here. What is the basic staff configuration?
8. Has that changed since you joined the staff?
9. What is your total compensation package?
10. How dependent are you on volunteers to do your job?
11. Who enlists your volunteers for you?
12. What is the system for the training of volunteers?
13. If you could make one change in the whole staff scene here, what would it be?
14. To whom are you accountable?
15. Are you a member of this religious tradition?
16. What will you be doing five years from now?
17. How much time do you spend on one-to-one meetings with the senior pastor in the typical week? That includes those two-minute corridor conversations.
18. What was your training or formal education to prepare you for your current role here?
19. What have you found to be your most helpful continuing education experiences?
20. What are the most attractive entry points for newcomers into the life of this congregation?
21. What is the system here for assimilating new people?
22. Who among the paid staff here clearly is the number one recipient of unreserved trust from the members?
23. How many hours a week do you spend at the computer?

24. Do you have your own secretary or do you share a secretary or do you do your own secretarial work?

25. When more help is needed, will this congregation (a) overload present staff, (b) hire additional staff, or (c) enlist volunteers?

I. The Pastor of a Nearby Congregation

1. Where were you before?
2. When did you come here?
3. What is the big difference between doing ministry here and where you were before?
4. Tell me about the congregation I am visiting.
5. Tell me about the religious subculture of this community.
6. Tell me about your congregation—origins, affiliation, attendance, staff, budget, do best, niche or special ministries, plans for the future.
7. Tell me about the pastor of the congregation I am visiting.
8. What is your point of greatest frustration in doing ministry here today?

J. Recent New Members (Adults)

In a forty-five-minute group interview with five to seventy adults who joined this congregation during the past three to twenty-four months, I advise them I want to ask only seven questions, but I may interrupt with more detailed follow-up questions at any point.

1. Do any of you have any questions about who I am, why I am here, or why you are in this gathering? Or has this been explained to you?
2. What is your name, and what brought you to this church originally? Why did you first come here?
3. Why did you return?
4. Why did you decide to join?
5. If you could wave a magic wand and make one change here, what would you change?
6. How well do each of you feel you have been assimilated into the life and fellowship of this congregation? On a scale of one to ten in which one is only a member, five is fairly well

assimilated, and ten is fully and completely assimilated, what is your number?

7. Finally, brag to me about what this congregation does best.

K. Ex-Members

In talking with former members who have not changed their place of residence, I ask three starter questions.

1. What brought you to that congregation originally?
2. Tell me about your involvement while you were a member.
3. Why did you leave, where did you go, and any other second thoughts on that whole sequence?

L. The Custodian

As the custodian walks me through the church plant, I usually begin with questions such as these:

1. What is the seating capacity of the worship center?
2. What will be the next big expenditure for maintenance here?
3. Do you have any serious needs for either additional or replacement equipment?
4. Are you able to stay on schedule on major maintenance?
5. What is your greatest point of frustration in what people here expect of you?
6. To whom are you accountable?
7. What is your best and most heavily used weekday meeting room?

M. Community Leaders

In talking with one or two community leaders for a half hour each, I ask five starter questions.

1. What is your role in this community?
2. If you came from another community, contrast here with there.
3. What is the essence of this community? What are the key social, economic, demographic, and political variables and how are they changing?
4. Who are the most visible and/or influential churches here?
5. Tell me about the church I am visiting.

4. The "Where Am I?" Questions

Earlier the need for the interventionist to keep asking, "Where am I?" was emphasized. This leads to a new set of questions that the interventionist asks both of others and also of himself or herself. These are designed to enable the interventionist to gain a reasonably accurate description of contemporary reality.

Most planning models require a realistic description of contemporary reality. For example, one three-step model begins with (1) a vision of a new tomorrow, (2) a description of contemporary reality, and (3) a strategy that will make it possible to move from here to there. In other words, it is difficult to map out a route to a desired destination without knowing the destination and the starting point. Congregations that are simply drifting in a goalless manner into the future do not find it especially useful to identify either the destination nor the beginning point called contemporary reality.

A. The Theological Stance

1. Where is this congregation on that theological spectrum that runs from fundamentalism on the far right through conservative, postconservative,[1] evangelical, the middle-of-the-theological road to various stages of liberalism on the left?

2. Where is the pastor on the spectrum?

3. Where are the recent new members on this spectrum?

4. Where are the current influential leaders on this spectrum?

5. If this is a denominationally affiliated congregation, is it to the theological right or the theological left of what is the dominant position of that denomination?

6. Has this congregation moved to the theological left or right of where it was twenty years ago? Why?

7. Is it to the theological right or left of the theological seminaries that it supports and/or from which it draws staff?

8. Is worship primarily experiential or presentational?

9. Is the number one priority in worship here to exalt the first, the second, or the third person of the Holy Trinity? What do the prayers, the hymns, the sermon, and the other teachings suggest?[2]

10. What appears to be the dominant theme in the preaching? (Examples include grace, spiritual warfare, hope, teaching, a challenge to accept Jesus Christ as Lord and Savior, love, the gifts of the Spirit, current social or political issues, missions, and autobiographical stories by the preacher.)

B. The Basic Trends

1. What has been the trend over the past ten years in the average worship attendance? Why?
2. What has been the trend over the past twenty or thirty years in the average Sunday school attendance? Why?
3. What has been the trend over the past dozen years in the number of new members received annually? Why?
4. Has the average number of new members joining by letter of transfer annually during the past dozen years exceeded, by at least a two-to-one ratio, the number lost by letter of transfer?
5. Has the number of new members received annually by baptism and/or profession of faith exceeded, by at least a two-to-one ratio, the number lost by death?
6. Has the annual number of baptisms of all ages been equal to at least 3 percent of the total membership?
7. How many new members are needed each year simply to replace those who die, drop out, move away, or transfer their membership to another congregation? 3 percent? 7 percent? 9 percent? 12 percent? 20 percent? Why?
8. Has the median age of the confirmed membership increased or decreased during the past decade?
9. Does this congregation own at least one acre of land for every one hundred people at worship on the typical weekend?
10. Do the average weekly contributions from living members equal at least twenty dollars times the average weekly worship attendance?
11. Was the total amount of member contributions in 1996 approximately double the total for 1980—the increase required to offset inflation?
12. Is the number of church-owned off-street parking spaces equal to at least 50 percent of the attendance at the most heavily attended worship service?

13. What has been the average length of pastorates here since 1960?

14. Has the system for the assimilation of new members been expanded to match the rate of numerical growth in membership and attendance?

15. Is this congregation completing one chapter in its ministry? Or is it about to begin a new chapter in the same volume? Or is it ready to begin a new volume? Or is it immobilized between chapters?

C. Worship and Music

1. Is the approch to the corporate worship of God here primarily a presentational style or more of a participatory style?

2. Is it formal, informal, moderately liturgical, or highly liturgical?

3. What is the age-group or generation for whom this worship experience was designed?

4. How frequently is Holy Communion offered?

5. How many worship experiences are scheduled for the typical weekend?

6. Are they largely carbon copies? Or is one service clearly designed for a specific constituency while another is designed for a different constituency?

7. Is the reliance on instrumental music largely on acoustic sound or electronic sound? (This may be the most significant generational difference in music.)

8. How much time elapses between the beginning of the worship service and the sermon? (The basic generalization is that the larger the crowd, the longer that period of time before the sermon.)

9. How long is the sermon? Is the length consistent with the central theme or themes of the preaching here? Is the length consistent with the size of the crowd? (The basic generalization is that the larger the crowd and/or the greater the emphasis on teaching, the longer the sermon.)

10. How many preachers on the typical weekend?

11. What is the pace of the service? (The basic generalization is that the smaller the crowd and/or the older the worshipers, the slower the pace.)

12. Is the primary constituency for the typical worship here the members or first-time visitors? How does the design reflect that priority?

13. What appears to be the dress code for people coming to worship here? Are there clear generational differences? Is this a problem?

14. Who is the worship leader? The preacher? An associate minister? A lay volunteer? A worship leader team? The choir director? A song leader? The minister of prayer? Whoever is available?

15. Is there an adult chancel choir? If yes, does it sing an anthem? Or is it a background group for the worship leader team? If there is no adult chancel choir, does that appear to be a significant omission? If there is an adult chancel choir, how many voices? Is that the number you would expect here? What proportion are male?

16. How many announcements are made? Who makes them? When? Is the content directed largely to members? Or largely to visitors?

17. Is the schedule designed to encourage a summer slump in attendance? (At least 15 percent of all Protestant congregations on the North American continent encourage a summer slump by (a) cutting back on the number of Sunday school classes and/or (b) cutting back on the ministry of music and/or (c) scheduling guest preachers and/or (d) reducing the number of worship experiences on the weekend and/or (e) cutting back on the weekday programing and/or (f) meeting in another room while the worship center is being renovated. This is most common in those congregations that are strongly member oriented since two-thirds of all two-generation families that change their place of residence do so during the summer.)

18. Are children encouraged to be in worship for the entire service?

19. How many *different* services are offered on Christmas Eve?

20. Who greets the worshipers as they leave following that worship service?

21. How long does it take to empty the room following the benediction?

D. The Level of Commitment

Most Christian congregations write a self-fulfilling prophecy. At one end of the spectrum are the churches that create a high commitment congregation by projecting high expectations of people in general and members in particular. At the other end of that spectrum are the congregations that project low expectations of people.

1. Does the Sunday schedule project the expectation that people will be present for one, two, three, four, five, or six periods of time?

2. Does the Sunday morning schedule encourage parents to be in worship while their children are in Sunday school?

3. Is the primary goal of the Sunday morning schedule to accommodate the person who wants (a) to participate in an adult class, (b) to teach in the children's Sunday school, and (c) to attend worship?

4. What is the ratio of worship attendance to membership? (In high commitment congregations worship attendance normally exceeds the confirmed membership while in low commitment churches that ratio is under 50 percent.)

5. What is the ratio of average Sunday school attendance to average worship attendance?

6. What are the requirements for becoming a full member?

7. How long is the class offered for adults contemplating becoming members? Eight sessions? Sixteen session? Thirty sessions? Forty-five sessions?

8. How many continuing classes and study groups are offered for adults?

9. How difficult is it to remove a person's name from the membership roster?

10. What training is required of volunteers before they can fill a volunteer role here?

11. What proportion of the members are tithers?

12. What proportion of total receipts are allocated for benevolences?

E. Member or Outreach Oriented?

1. Does the local climate suggest the top priority here is taking care of the members or identifying, reaching, attracting, serving, and assimilating tomorrow's future members?

2. Which slices of the local population probably would not feel at home here?

3. What does the Sunday morning bulletin suggest?

4. What does the real estate suggest?

5. What does the design of the worship experience suggest?

6. What appear to be the major barriers to reaching younger adults?

F. Administrative and Leadership Issues

1. Who is the number one visionary or initiating leader here? The pastor? A trustee? A lay elder? The board?

2. Does the necessary administrative work get done and is it completed on time?

3. Who carries the final responsibility for the overall administration of this parish?

4. What is the internal system for accountability and performance?

5. What is the quality of the system for internal communication here? What is the extent of the redundancy in that system?

G. Public Relations and Advertising

1. What are the channels of communication used by this congregation to reach potential future members? Televsion? Direct mail? Special events? Radio? The Yellow Pages? Newspapers? Paid staff? Billboards? The telephone? Door-to-door visitation? Trained volunteers?

2. How narrowly and precisely is that future constituency defined?

3. How does the content of the messages that are sent match the characteristics and needs of that constituency?

4. How effective is the current system?

H. What Are the Sources of Identity?

For most of the history of Christianity on the North American continent, the vast majority of congregations found their identity in one or more of these four sources.

1. The people. One example was the nationality or language or racial heritage. The Norwegian Lutheran, the Italian

Methodist, the Swedish Baptist, the Dutch Reformed, and the German Lutheran churches were highly visible examples of this. An even clearer contemporary example is the Black Baptist or the Korean Presbyterian congregation. As one scholar has pointed out, for American-born blacks, race is a more powerful source of identity than nationality or denomination.[3]

Other congregations found part of their identity as a "working class church" or "the church that attracts the movers and shakers in this town" or as the "university church." In recent years, the age of the current membership has become a source of identity as some congregations specialize in reaching young adults while others serve an aging constituency.

2. The denominational tie. In Wisconsin, Minnesota, and the Dakotas this may be described in negative terms. "We're the only non-Lutheran Protestant congregation in this end of the county." The Reorganized Church of Jesus Christ of the Latter Day Saints have had to explain to strangers that they are not the same as the Salt Lake City Mormons.

For tens of thousands of congregations, however, that denominational affiliation was the number one source of identity. This was and is true for Roman Catholics, Anglicans, Episcopalians, Seventh-day Adventists, the Latter-day Saints, the Christian Reformed, and others. It also was and is true for the majority of congregations affiliated with the Southern Baptist Convention, the United Methodists, the Presbyterian Church (USA), and several other traditions.

In recent years, however, the value of that denominational tie as a source of congregational identity has eroded. One reason was the decision in many denominational seminaries to change priorities. In the nineteenth century and the early years of the twentieth century, denominational seminaries actively sought to inculcate in students the distinctive ethos of that particular religious tradition. They upheld the doctrinal, confessional, and polity standards of that denomination and sought to transmit these to the students. All students were aggressively socialized into the belief system, the traditions, and the culture of that denomination. During the past several decades most theological seminaries affiliated with the mainline Protestant denominations have moved away from that stance. One scholar described that shift as "from inquiry about the nature and substance of the tradition to inquiry about the meaing and plausibility of the tradition in the modern world."[4]

The second half of the twentieth century popularized the slogan that a theological seminary should be "urban, ecumenical, and university related." In operational terms this has meant that (a) concerns about race, gender, and class should replace denominational traditions as the context for theological reflection, (b) the search for the truth should replace the confessions as the yardstick for the study of theology, (c) a focus on "the church in its wholeness" should replace the effort to transmit a distinctive denominational heritage, and (d) the seminary should abandon its role as both a reinforcer of denominational identity and as a channel to transmit to future generations of pastors the distinctive belief system, the traditions, the polity, and the patterns of worship of that denomination by accepting a new role in the "intellectual center of the church's life."

3. A geographical definition of the parish. In addition to the distinctive characteristics of the members and the denominational affiliation, a third source of identity was the territory served by that congregation. The pre-1960 concept of parish boundaries in the Roman Catholic Church in the United States was a highly visible example of that pattern. Far more numerous were the Protestant congregations that drew nine-tenths of their members from within an hour's walk of the meeting house.

4. The pastor. A fourth source of identity for many congregations was that highly visible and long-tenured pastor who was a prominent and influential leader in the community for two or three or four decades.

Literally thousands of congregations depended on two or three or four of these sources for their distinctive identity. Eventually, however, (a) the boats no longer bring tens of thousands of immigrants from Europe, (b) the first- and second-generation members move away or die, (c) their children and grandchildren identify themselves as Americans or Canadians without a hyphen, (d) the automobile encourages people to drive to church and the regional church replaces the neighborhood parish, (e) institutional loyalties, including denominational ties, no longer are passed along by inheritance, and (f) that well-known pastor retires to the west coast of Florida.

These changes raise a half dozen questions for the interventionist.

1. What were the sources of identity for this congregation when it was founded and in its early years?
2. What eroded those sources?
3. What replaced those eroded sources?
4. What are the current sources of identity?
5. What will be the useful sources ten years from now?
6. Who among the local leaders is concerned about this?

The new sources might be in such words and phrases as music, youth, evangelical, liberal, preaching, ministries with families, or a score of other sources. This discussion on identity leads into the next set of starter questions. What are the current entry points for newcomers? That, however, requires a larger perspective for analysis.

I. Static or Dynamic?

One of the most subtle questions to be explored by the interventionist concerns the approach to ministry. The basic alternatives can be described by a brief outline.

1. Does this congregation assume a static condition for their constituents or a dynamic status?

Static. The congregation will tend to use static categories such as youth, choirs, women, men, young adults, senior citizens, married couples, members, singles, families, and children as the basic building blocks for conceptualizing ministry. This approach is widely used in long-established congregations.

Dynamic. This approach assumes that everyone is on a journey and that people move through stages as the years pass. The conceptual framework used in designing a ministry identifies when and how that congregation will intervene in the journeys of people. This is more widely used in congregations seeking to reach adults without any active church relationship and less common in the member-oriented church. Three examples of a dynamic approach to intervention are these.

1. Life Cycle

The ministry plan is designed to minister to the needs of people at various points of the life cycle. That spectrum might include (a) an overnight retreat for newly engaged couples, (b) a weekend retreat for newlyweds both in their first marriage (54 percent of all weddings in the United States in 1990), (c) a weekend retreat for newlyweds where each had been married and divorced at least once previously (20 percent of all 1990 weddings), (d) a weekend retreat for newlyweds where one had never been married and the other had been divorced (22 percent of all 1990 weddings), (e) an overnight for couples expecting their first child, (f) an overnight for the parents in newly blended families, and (g) an all-day event for parents who have a baby not yet six months of age on the development processes of very young children. Two dozen other events and a dozen or more newly constituted continuing groups or classes could be added to that.

2. The Faith Journey

A different conceptual framework begins with the assumption that every adult is on a personal religious pilgrimage. At one end of that spectrum are the skeptics, searchers, agnostics, doubters, birthright Christians, and others who fit into a nonbeliever category. The next stages include believers, learners, disciples, and apostles.

The church seeks to intervene at the appropriate stage in the lives of individuals and this often will be different for the wife than the husband.

3. Attractive Entry Points

A third approach begins not with where people are on their journey, but rather with the resources of that congregation. It seeks to offer a smorgasbord of events, classes, choirs, mutual support groups, and so forth and hope that most will be attractive to both members and nonmembers.

This outline may stimulate questions such as these from the interventionist.

1. What is the basic conceptual framework for intervention here? Static? Dynamic?
2. What makes that work here?
3. If it is not working, why not?
4. Given the subculture of this congregation, is that the appropriate approach?
5. If not, should we try to introduce a different approach at this time? Or would that overload this system?
6. If it is not the appropriate approach, what must be done to introduce a different conceptual framework?
7. What is the gap between the perception of reality among the leaders here on this question and my perception of reality?
8. If it is the appropriate approach, what can be done to strengthen, undergird, reinforce, and improve it?
9. Who are the potential allies who can make that happen?
10. Is this a conceptual framework for diagnosis that can be used productively in this setting? Or should I seek a different conceptual framework that the leaders here would be more comfortable with in this process?

J. Trust or Distrust?

Perhaps the most subjective, but certainly one of the most timely sets of diagnostic questions concerns the issue of trust. This is a very serious issue in those denominational systems in which the primary role of denominational agencies is to function as a regulatory body. Is this congregation organized around trust or distrust?

The younger the current generation of influential leaders and/or the larger the size of the congregation and/or the faster the rate of numerical growth and/or the higher the level of formal educational attainment of the new members and/or the larger the proportion of individual entrepreneurs among the new members and/or the higher the income level of the members and/or the greater the degree of diversity within the membership and/or the larger the proportion of the total workload carried by volunteers and the smaller the proportion carried by paid staff, the greater the need for the congregation to function on a high level of trust and to encourage lay initiative.

One part of the explanation for the recent emergence of scores of very large independent churches is that many of them have found it easy to create a congregational culture that is based on unreserved trust of the lay leadership and encouraged lay initiative. One part of the explanation for the recent numerical decline of several mainline Protestant denominations is that culture is built on a distrust of local leadership and a response to the perceived need for the denomination to function as a regulatory body.[5]

This discussion raises a half dozen starter questions for the interventionist.

1. In its approach to ministry, is this congregation predominantly staff driven or is it largely driven by lay initiatives?

2. If it is largely staff or pastor driven, is that compatible with the denominational culture?

3. If it is largely lay initiative, is the denominational culture supportive of that emphasis?

4. If the denominational culture is based heavily on distrust of congregational leadership, what limitations does that place on the scenarios for tomorrow? (For example, is this congregation institutionally free to unilaterally launch five or ten or forty off-campus ministries during the next decade?)[6]

5. If the denominational culture is organized around distrust of congregational leadership, but this congregation is exceptionally open to lay initiatives, how do we explain that contradiction? Why is that possible here? Can it continue?

6. Frequently the level of trust and the openness to influential lay initiatives reflect the leadership style of a long-tenured pastor. Is that true here? If yes, what will happen when the current pastor leaves?

Too often this issue of trust is discussed in terms of personalities, but to a substantial degree it is a systemic issue. Is that system, and especially that subsystem called internal communication, designed to build trust or to undermine trust?

K. Shaping the Future

1. What now appear to be the distinctive characteristics of the

people that this congregation should be serving a dozen years from now?

2. Is this a functionally useful building on a good site at a good location that can be used by this congregation to serve its anticipated future constituencies in the year 2025?

3. If you were going to organize a new congregation to serve that predicted future constituency, would you choose this location and/or design a building resembling this one?

4. Is the current pastor or senior minister fully accepted here? Or did the current pastor come to fill a vacancy that does not really exist? Or is the current pastor an unintentional interim minister?

5. Is the current pastor a good match for this congregation as of 1980? Or today? Or 2010?

6. Has a future constituency been identified? Or is the operational assumption that tomorrow's new members will be largely carbon copies of today's members?

7. In terms of program amd ministry, is this congregation prepared to reach and serve a new constituency during the next dozen years?

8. If not, what changes must be made? Or is the current operating assumption that 80 percent of today's members will still be here a dozen years hence?

9. Which congregations now in existence already are competing to serve that constituency?

10. What will be the most effective channels of communication for reaching new constituencies during the next dozen years?

11. What changes in the staffing configuration will be required to reach new constituencies in the years ahead? Which staff positions will need to be redefined?

12. Is this congregation prepared to make those staffing changes?

13. If this is a denominationally affiliated congregation, what changes will be required in that denominational system to facilitate the process of this congregation reaching and serving new constituencies in the years ahead?

14. Will a change in the role of the governing board be needed to serve a new constituency in a new era?

15. Will it be necessary to raise the level of financial contribu-

tions from the members in order to pay the costs of reaching a new constituency?

16. Is the current name of this congregation an asset or a liability?

17. Are the internal criteria for self-evaluation consistent with and supportive of efforts to reach a new constituency?

18. If this is a denominationally affiliated congregation, are the denominational criteria for the evaluation of congregations supportive of this church's role for the future?

CAUTION

The questions presented in this chapter should not be viewed as a complete inventory! They are offered only to illustrate a sample of the possibilities and to distinguish between the starter and the follow-up questions. Every interventionist will want to build an inventory of questions that is consistent with the role and style of that person's approach.

The big omission from this array consists of the questions to be raised in specialized areas such as church finances, missions, building programs, potential new ministries, staffing, and community outreach. Those questions usually must be tailored to fit that specific set of local circumstances.[7]

To state it even more simply, these are some of the several hundred questions I have used as a parish consultant. This is not a complete list, but it does illustrate the range. During the past three and one-half decades, I have worked with congregations on three continents that cover the middle 90 percent of the theological spectrum. They have helped me define contemporary reality in each congregation, they have evoked the follow-up questions that often are more revealing than the initial starter questions, and they have been useful in my role as a diagnostician.

Please feel free to pick and choose, to amend and rephrase, but most important of all, to generate new questions as you build your personal inventory of the questions needed by the intentional interventionist.

CHAPTER TWELVE

What Happened to the Context?

In 1950 life was relatively simple. Most ministers served as pastors of worshiping communities. Denominational agencies enlisted committed Christians to serve as missionaries in other parts of the world and provided financial support and oversight for their ministry. Teenagers deferred to adult role models as they planned their future. Congregations, and occasionally denominational agencies, sponsored weeklong revivals. The vast majority of parish pastors lived in church-owned housing. Only a small proportion of women married to pastors were employed outside the home. Every Sunday morning millions of adults walked to church. The farm population numbered 25 million, down 21 percent from thirty years earlier. Denominational publishing houses produced the hymnals, educational materials, books, and magazines used by members of their religious traditions. The vast majority of seminary graduates became parish pastors. For many, the one-car garage attached to the single-family house was a luxury. Governments at all levels displayed genuine respect for organized religion. The threat of world communism was the central organizing principle for American foreign policy. Sunday school attendance was growing so rapidly that many churches had to construct a new building to house the growth. A total of 21.2 million cows produced 116 billion pounds of milk on American farms.

Protestant Christianity was about to enter into a decade of explosive numerical growth. Sixteen denominations started two-thirds of all new congregations in the United States in 1950. The very large independent or nondenominational congregation was a rarity. During the next fifteen years, various denominational systems would build another group of new institutions (theological seminaries, homes, camps, retreat centers, and so forth). A journey of ten miles to work was perceived as a long commuting distance. Akron, Ohio, was the place to go to study an emerging phenomenon subsequently described as the megachurch. Forty-three percent of all American men, age sixty-five and over, were employed in the labor force. Slightly over 32 percent of the American population, age twenty-five and over, had completed four years of high school including the 6 percent who had completed four years of college. Fewer than one million American families earned the equivalent of $60,000 annually in terms of the 1994 dollar. Except for their work with students, parachurch organizations had practically no visibility in North America. When they needed help in fund-raising, congregations usually turned to a denominational staff person. Three of the fastest growing vocations in the labor force were church secretary, director of Christian education, and associate minister. Four-fifths of the 250,000 legal immigrants into the United States in 1950 came from Europe. Denominational systems were the basic building blocks for interchurch cooperation and for ecumenical ventures. Pastors expected the denominational pension system would be the central source of their income in retirement. Every year brought an increase in the numbers of paid staff members in national denominational agencies and regional judicatories. English was the language spoken by nearly all the visitors to the national parks. Nearly all the very large congregations in California carried a denominational label.

TWO ERAS LATER

By the closing years of the twentieth century, the social and ecclesiastical scene had become vastly more complicated. The majority of ordained ministers were not serving as full-time parish pastors. Theological seminaries were expected to serve as therapy centers, to help those on a religious pilgrimage discover their identity, to train people as counselors, to prepare students planning to go on to graduate school, to help mature adults find a new vocation, and to train people for the parish ministry.

The majority of North Americans serving as missionaries in other parts of the world were related to a parachurch agency.

The majority of teenagers relied on peers for counsel and direction. Parachurch agencies scheduled huge revivals attracting tens of thousands of participants, with Promise Keepers the most highly visible new example. The housing allowance, with its attractive double deduction, was replacing the church-owned residence for the pastor. The regional church was replacing the neighborhood church. Approximately 35 million of the regular church attenders of 1950, including the majority of the "church pillars," had died by the end of 1995. The farm population in the United States in 1990 was 4.6 million, down 70 percent from the 15.7 million of 1960. Five years later the United States Bureau of the Census announced that the farm population had dwindled to the point that it no longer would be counted. A rapidly growing number of congregations were turning to parachurch organizations and commercial agencies for resources in music, teaching materials, books, and periodicals. Perhaps as many as one-third to one-half of all the seminary graduates of 1995 will spend at least fifteen years as a full-time parish pastor. In 1990 70 percent of all new single-family homes constructed in the United States included an attached two- or three-car garage. The decision by the United States Supreme Court to read into the Establishment Clause of the Constitution the phrase "wall of separation between church and state" opened the door to an increasingly adversarial relationship between church and government in the United States—and added one more reason why many Canadians are happy they live north of the border.

In 1995 sixteen million American households had an income of $60,000 or more. In 1990 several denominations reported their average Sunday school attendance was below 50 percent of the 1960 total, and empty classrooms were being remodeled into offices for staff. In 1992 in the United States 9.9 million cows produced 152 billion pounds of milk. Most of the mainline Protestant denominations in both the United States and Canada were reporting a net decrease in the number of members. The majority of new congregations started were planted by existing churches, the newer denominations, or by independent entrepreneurial pastors. The number of independent megachurches was greater than the combined total of megachurches carrying a Methodist, Anglican, Presbyterian (PCUSA), Lutheran, United Church of Canada, Episcopal, or United Church of Christ label. Only 10 percent of the 1.5 million immigrants into the United States in 1990 came from Europe. Pastors and congregations have become the basic building blocks for most new inter-church and ecumenical ventures. At least a dozen denominations have been announcing substantial cutbacks in the number of paid staff in both regional and national agencies. English is one of several languages heard in the national parks in the United States and Canada. In 1990 only 17 percent of all first-time brides in the United States were teenagers compared to 42 percent as recently as 1970. Orange County, California, Harris County, Texas, and central Oklahoma had become the places to visit for those interested in studying the modern megachurch. Between 1974 and 1996, the population of the United States increased by 23 percent, but the number of telephone numbers doubled (partly because of the increase in the number of congregations calling for help). Among the occupations and job titles reporting shrinking numbers were bank tellers, directors of Christian education, roustabouts, switchboard operators, church secretaries, typesetters, associate pastors, and farmers. In 1993, 80 percent of the American population, age twenty-five and over, had completed at least four years of high school, including the 22 percent who had completed at least four years of college. Only 16 percent of all American males, age 65 and over, were employed in 1990.

CREATING A VACUUM

These and hundreds of other changes have drastically altered the context for doing ministry in the early years of the twenty-first century. They also have radically changed the relationships between congregations and denominational systems. A dozen of these have combined to create a series of vacuums.

1. The erosion of inherited denominational loyalties, the sharp reduction in the number of immigrants from Europe, the replacement of the place of residence by vocation as the founda-

tion stone for building one's personal social network, the increased geographical separation of the place of residence from the place of work, recreation, shopping, and worship, the increase in the number of interfaith, interdenominational, and interracial marriages, the rise in the level of expectations people bring to church, the demand by people born after World War II for high quality, the increase in the number of charges of sexual misconduct filed against the clergy, the declining influence of the public schools, the increasingly pluralistic nature of society (especially in Canada), and the obsolescence of the accepted norms of the 1950s have greatly increased the complexity of congregational life.

2. The changes mentioned above, especially the decrease in inherited denominational loyalties, and the demand for relevance and quality have sharply increased the level of competition among the churches for new members. It is not unusual for either disenchanted members or newcomers to the community to "shop" five to ten congregations before deciding on a new church home.

3. The emergence of a couple of thousand megachurches with seven-day-a-week ministries also has raised the level of competence required of ministers and lay staff members.

4. That dramatic rise in the level of educational attainment of the American people opened the door to the concept of utilizing the services of an intentional interventionist. The proportion of college graduates in the adult population quadrupled in forty-three years—and many of the volunteer congregational leaders now use professional consultants in their place of employment. In 1994, the world's largest consulting firms collected $18 billion in consultation fees and the total income of the consulting industry was double that. Every year at least 7,000 Protestant congregations in the United States hire a consultant who is not a member of their denominational staff.

5. While it is rarely mentioned, one of the most persuasive arguments for the use of the professional interventionist is the work of the county agricultural agents. In four decades in the middle of the twentieth century, they transformed American agriculture from labor intensive and low productivity to capital

intensive and very high productivity. Between 1920 and 1995, the number of farmers in the United States dropped by 95 percent and the production of wheat, corn, and milk more than doubled. With the research support of the United States Department of Agriculture and the land grant universities, they demonstrated the impact of research-based, planned intervention. (Is it too late for a partnership of denominational systems, theological seminaries, "Church Champions," and congregational leaders to replicate that model of intervention?)

6. Television has radically altered people's definition of "effective communication." This has affected preaching, worship, the teaching ministries, advertising, and internal communication.

7. The paving of millions of acres of land for highways and parking lots has encouraged people to drive, rather than walk, to their destination and to expect a convenient and safe parking space at the end of the journey.

8. The competition for the charitable dollar is far greater than it was in the 1950s.

9. At least a dozen large denominations report that congregations are forwarding a shrinking proportion of their total receipts to national headquarters.

10. There is a growing recognition that the old assumption that "one size fits all" no longer is a valid approach to servicing congregations. The combination of (a) the increase in the complexity of congregational life, (b) the arrival of new generations of churchgoers who bring a different set of expectations to church than were brought by earlier generations, and (c) the rise in the level of competition among the churches means prescriptions must be customized to fit that unique set of circumstances. The role of national and regional denominational organizations as program agencies is shrinking rapidly.

11. Following the normal, natural, and predictable tendencies of mature bureaucracies in an affluent culture, several denominational systems have drifted in the direction of placing their regulatory role at the top of their priorities, ahead of resourcing congregations.[1]

12. When this priority on a regulatory role is combined with a

shrinkage in resources, one result is most denominational systems, both nationally and regionally, have been forced to cut back on the services they can provide to individual congregations.

One product of these and related changes has been to fuel the conviction, first widely articulated in the 1960s, that North Americans are now living in a "postdenominational era." This conviction is more widely shared west of the Mississippi River than east of it, so it is not surprising that many of the national conferences to discuss the implications are held west of that big river.[2]

Perhaps less visible, but far more significant, has been another consequence of these changes. That has been the creation of a vacuum and the identity of those who have moved to fill that vacuum. The number one example of this is illustrated by the deaths of the estimated 35 million regular churchgoers of 1950, most of whom were born before 1915. As the mainline Protestant denominations and their congregations continued to concentrate on reaching and serving Anglo adults born in the first half of the twentieth century, that created a vacuum. Who will be responsive to the religious needs of the generations born after 1950 and to the new immigrants?

One answer was the newer "made-in-America" denominations (see chapter 7), the Southern Baptist Convention, and that rapidly growing array of nondenominational churches. Overlapping that was the rediscovery of an evangelistic principle followed in the second half of the nineteenth century. The most effective way to reach new generations of North American–born residents and new immigrants from other parts of this planet is to invite them to help pioneer the creation of new congregations. That has produced the most highly visible example of filling the vacuum. That is in new church development. As the mainline Protestant denominations cut back by 60 to 95 percent from their level of new church development of the 1950s, that gap was filled by the newer denominations, by individual congregations, by independent groups, and by the Southern Baptist Convention.[3] (During the 1890s the Southern Baptist Convention started an average of approximately 400 new missions each year. A century later, the average had tripled to 1,300 a year. One factor behind that cutback in new church development in several mainline denominations was the diversion of resources to denominational mergers and issue-centered ministries.)

Another example of filling the vacuum is in music. For the first six decades of the twentieth century, congregational leaders and denominational systems were the chief sources of the new music for the churches. The birth of the contemporary Christian music movement coincided with the emergence of the Jesus People. The next stage was the creation of an informal new partnership including the new Christian music, the entertainment industry, a variety of parachurch organizations, the pioneers in contemporary worship, and scores of creative Christian entrepreneurs. That partnership spoke in meaningful terms to a new generation of churchgoers born after 1950.

The least visible, but a rapidly growing response to the vacuum created by the change in the priorities of denominational systems is the recent rapid growth in the number of financially endowed parishes. Since 1985 this movement has had the highest visibility in the Episcopal Church. It is possible the endowed parishes will become the research and development centers for North American Christianity in the twenty-first century. One example of that is the differences in the definition of the word *stewardship.* That word does not have the same meaning in the struggling congregations averaging eighty-five at worship as it carries in the endowed parish!

For many readers of this book, the most significant response to that vacuum consists of two trends. One is the growing demand by congregational leaders for resources. The other is the rapidly growing number of parachurch organizations, individual entrepreneurs, commercial agencies, parish consultants, musicians, architects, fund-raisers, theological schools, specialists in conflict management, consulting firms, church growth experts, writers, public relations specialists, magazines, electronic data processing companies, private publishing houses, bookstores, church-related colleges, and evangelists who are now available to fill that vacuum.

For those of us who are not ready to write off denominational systems as completely obsolete, the most exciting response to this vacuum is the redefinition of their primary role by several regional judicatories.[4] The leaders in these regional judicatories have largely or completely abandoned their role as program agencies. They also have abandoned the assumption that "one size fits all" in writing prescriptions for individual congregations. This has eliminated the need for huge regional rallies. The new role calls for the regional judicatory to (1) help congregations design a customized strategy for tomorrow's ministry, (2) challenge congregational leaders to do what they know they cannot do, and (3) resource congregations to enable them to implement that customized strategy.

As recently as 1970 the three major commercial networks served well over 90 percent of all American television viewers. By the late 1990s, their share of the market had dropped to 60 percent. A parallel, but perhaps even greater, change is occurring in the resourcing of congregations. In the 1950s the vast majority of Christian congregations in North America turned only to their denominational headquarters for resources. Today at least two-thirds turn to other sources for at least part of what they purchase. That trend is expanding the market for interventionists.

Tomorrow's Market for Interventionists

What will be the demand for professional interventionists in the churches in the twenty-first century? A reasonable guess is that by 2025 it will be at least five times the demand it was back in 1995. Who will service that market? The best answer is no one knows. A second best answer is a growing variety of venturesome and creative people. A reasonable guess is in the year 2025 a congregation will be able to turn to any one of these twenty-one possibilities. They are not ranked in order of availability!

1. Church Champions serving on the staff of a regional judicatory of a denomination.

2. The individual interventionist who works alone in a thrifty organizational context.

3. The parish consultant on the staff of a Christian college or university.

4. The professional interventionist who is on the staff of an architectural firm specializing in working with religious organizations.

5. The professional partnership of three to seven interventionists.

6. The parish consultant on the staff of a commercial fundraising organization.

7. The bivocational minister who spends one-third to one-half of the month serving as pastor of a small church and the rest of the month as a specialist in intervention.

8. The career intentional interim minister serving churches from several different religious traditions.

9. The part-time staff specialist in a large congregation who also is a part-time parish consultant.

10. The staff member of an endowed parish who spends 90 percent of the year serving as a parish consultant to other congregations.

11. The ex-pastor who is now a graduate student in a research university and is making a living as a part-time parish consultant.

12. The parish consultant on the staff of a national denominational agency.

13. The pastor who chooses early retirement to serve as a parish consultant.

14. The secular consulting firm that has identified congregations as potentially significant clients.

15. The parachurch organization that offers continuing educational experiences for congregational leaders, consultation services, publications, CD-ROM instructional disks, resources in music, expertise in fundraising, and other services to congregations.

16. The retreat center that has one or two parish consultants on the staff.

17. The staff member of a pastoral counseling center who also is a specialist in conflict resolution or in working with dysfunctional organizations.

18. The coalition of very large congregations with a joint staff that includes (a) a minister of missions, (b) a minister of lay training, and (c) a parish consultant. This coalition could consist of nine congregations in five different states.

19. The ex-wife of a parish pastor who is now a full-time professional parish consultant with a specialty in one phase of congregational life.

20. The parish consultant on the staff of a publishing house who also is a part-time editor.

21. The seminary professor who is a part-time parish consultant, perhaps while serving in a part-time role as a teacher in a seminary extension center.

Which of these possibilities do you believe will provide the most jobs for interventionists in congregational life in 2025? This observer's guess is categories 1, 8, 15, 7, 2, 9, 4, 5, 17, and 18 and perhaps in that order.

NOTES

Introduction

1. For an excellent, brief, and profound introduction to the religious scene in Canada, see Reginald W. Bibby, *There's Got to Be More*! (Winfield, B. C.: Wood Lakes Books, 1995). In this thoughtful volume, Bibby combines diagnosis and relevant prescriptions.

1. Who Are the Interventionists?

1. This is the central theme of Lyle E. Schaller, *The Change Agent* (Nashville: Abingdon Press, 1977) and Lyle E. Schaller, *Strategies For Change* (Nashville: Abingdon Press, 1993).

2. This is a central theme in Lincoln Caplan, *Skadden: Power, Money, and the Rise of a Legal Empire* (New York: Farrar Straus Girouxs, 1993).

2. What Baggage Do You Carry?

1. For a brief introduction to generational theory, see Lyle E. Schaller, *Reflections of a Contrarian* (Nashville: Abingdon Press, 1989), pp. 65-95.

2. This observer's experience suggests the best of the small congregations follow a different central organizing principle from that of large churches. See Lyle E. Schaller, *The Small Membership Church* (Nashville: Abingdon Press, 1994), pp. 23-29.

3. This observer's reflections on the value of using worship attendance to measure size can be found in Lyle E. Schaller, *Looking in the Mirror* (Nashville: Abingdon Press, 1984), pp. 14-37.

4. For one perspective on this, see Lyle E. Schaller, *44 Ways to Expand the Teaching Ministry of Your Church* (Nashville: Abingdon Press, 1992).

5. For a more extensive discussion on the size of groups, see Lyle E. Schaller, *Effective Church Planning* (Nashville: Abingdon Press, 1979), pp. 17-64.

6. While the basic trend in American society since the 1920s has been in the direction of increasing the choices open to people (education, employment, marriage, housing, health care, retail trade, transportation, entertainment, morality, travel, church relationship, food, and so forth), that trend does carry price tags. Some of these price tags are discussed in a provocative book on urban life. Alan Ehrenhalt, *The Lost City* (New York: Basic Books, 1995). One cost of choices has been the loss of a geographical definition of community. A second has been the erosion of authority.

4. What Do You Bring?

1. Geoffrey M. Bellman, *The Consultant's Calling: Bringing Who You Are to What You Do* (San Francisco: Jossey-Bass Publishers, 1990), pp. 127-43. Another useful background book is Gordon Lippitt and Ronald Lippitt, *The Consulting Process in Action* (La Jolla, Calif.: University Associates, 1978).

2. The questionnaire approach to intervention is by far the most sophisticated method and requires an exceptionally high level of technical competence. Unless the phrasing of the questions and the interpretation of the responses are of very high quality, the result may be more harm than help. The opening statement in a public debate on the validity of standardized questionnaires can be found in R. C. Lewontin, "Sex, Lies, and Social Science," *New York Review of Books*, April 20, 1995, pp. 24-29. The first of several responses is by Edward O. Laumann, et al. "Sex, Lies, and Social Science: An Exchange," *The New York Review of Books*, May 25, 1995, pp. 43-44. This provocative dialogue is an accessible resource to those who want to weigh the value of standardized questionnaires.

3. For an example of a candidate arriving early in order to be fully prepared to ask informed questions of the pulpit nominating committee, see William M. Stark, "A Multi-Cultural Church in a Multi-Cultural Community," in Lyle E. Schaller, ed., *Center City Churches* (Nashville: Abingdon Press, 1993), pp. 100-03.

4. The secular periodicals I have found to be most useful include: *The Atlantic Monthly, The Wilson Quarterly, The Harvard Business Review, Wired, Early Childhood Connections, Change, The Public Interest, Society, College Board Review, The New Republic, Phi Delta Kappan, American Demographics, Fortune, The Economist, Current,* and *Harpers.*

5. For a long and provocative discussion of this issue, see Francis Fukuyama, *Trust* (New York: The Free Press, 1995). This book picks up on the observations of Alexis de Tocqueville about the unique role of voluntary associations in the American culture. One of Fukuyama's central themes is that healthy voluntary associations can be built only on unreserved trust of the people and that also is the foundation for liberal democracy.

6. What Are the Lines of Demarcation?

1. This distinction between first commandment and second commandment congregations is a central theme of Lyle E. Schaller, *The Small Membership Church* (Nashville: Abingdon Press, 1994).

2. A superb book on exclusion and inclusion is Vivian Gussin Paley, *You Can't Say You Can't Play* (Cambridge, Ma.: Harvard University Press, 1992). It should be required reading for parents of young children, pastors of small congregations, kindergarten and first grade teachers, counselors with junior high youth groups, adults who were first-born children, and those who take Leviticus 19:34 seriously.

3. This distinction between active and passive congregations is described in

Lyle E. Schaller, *Activating the Passive Church* (Nashville: Abingdon Press, 1981), pp. 40-70.

4. Additional suggestions for overcoming complacency are described in Lyle E. Schaller, *Strategies for Change* (Nashville: Abingdon Press, 1993), pp. 38-124. Also see Lyle E. Schaller, *44 Steps Up Off the Plateau* (Nashville: Abingdon Press, 1993).

7. European or American?

1. While it is written from the perspective of the nonbeliever, a useful book on the American religious culture is Harold Bloom, *The American Religion* (New York: Simon & Schuster, 1992).

2. A brief but incisive editorial on the Americanization of a European religious heritage is John Suk, "The CRC's Sticking Points," *The Banner*, June 19, 1995, p. 2.

3. While the answer is clear to any serious student of the Holy Scriptures, this book will not stray into the current debate over whether or not an orthodox, Southern Baptist Christian must, by definition, be a five-point Calvinist.

4. A provocative brief explanation of why Afrocentrism is so important to American-born blacks in search of identity in a highly individualistic American culture is Gerald Early, "Understanding Afrocentrism," *Civilization*, July/August 1995, pp. 31-39. The response to the verdict in the O. J. Simpson trial in October 1995 illustrated, that from an Afrocentric perspective, race is a more significant line of demarcation than class, gender, citizenship, or education. Early's essay also helps to explain why it may be difficult for a Eurocentric theological seminary to recruit and train American-born blacks to go out and organize new Afrocentric congregations that will feel strong loyalties to a European religious heritage. For a more comprehensive review of this general subject, see C. Eric Lincoln and Lawrence H. Mamiya, *The Black Church in the African American Experience* (Durham, N.C.: Duke University Press, 1990), pp. 382-404.

5. A related line of demarcation is that many of the worshipers in Afrocentric and made-in-America congregations are rhythm-endowed while many who come from a Eurocentric religious heritage are rhythm-impaired. The former usually clap on the upbeat while the latter clap on the downbeat of the music. For a provocative argument in support of the role of rhythm in building community, see William H. McNeil, *Keeping Together in Time* (Cambridge, Ma.: Harvard University Press, 1995). McNeil's thesis helps to explain the generalization that the larger the size of the congregation and/or the younger the people and/or the higher the level of anonymity among those present, the more important music is.

6. One author has argued that it was not until the 1920s that the United States freed itself from a European cultural domination. Ann Douglas, *Terrible Honesty* (New York: Farrar, Straus & Giroux, 1995). A liberal author traces that emancipation back to the nineteenth century. Michael Kazin, *The Populist Persuasion* (New York: Basic Books, 1995).

8. *Seventeen Syndromes*

1. See the description of the collie-sized congregation in Lyle E. Schaller, *Looking in the Mirror* (Nashville: Abingdon Press, 1984), pp. 14-18.

2. Ibid., pp. 21-24.

3. Ibid., pp. 27-29.

4. The complacent congregation is described in more detail in Lyle E. Schaller, *Strategies for Change* (Nashville: Abingdon Press, 1993), pp. 38-40.

5. For an exceptional essay on the barriers to change, see John P. Kotter, "Leading Change: Why Transformation Efforts Fail," *Harvard Business Review*, March/April 1995, pp. 59-67. Kotter emphasizes that "establishing a sense of urgency" is the first step in transforming any organization.

6. One example of the new model is described by Michael E. Porter, "The Competitive Advantage of the Inner City," *Harvard Business Review*, May/June 1995, pp. 55-71.

7. See Lyle E. Schaller, "It's Not a Business!" *Looking in the Mirror* (Nashville: Abingdon Press, 1984), pp. 38-58.

9. *What Are the Central Organizing Principles?*

1. For one example of anti-Catholicism as an organizing principle in one denomination, see Robert Moats Miller, *Bishop G. Bromley Oxnam: Paladin of Liberal Protestantism* (Nashville: Abingdon Press, 1990), pp. 398-444.

2. Robert Wuthnow, *Christianity in the 21st Century* (New York: Oxford University Press, 1993), p. 134.

10. *Evangelism or Intervention?*

1. An informative account of how one congregation reversed a period of numerical decline is Randy Frazee, *The Come Back Congregation* (Nashville: Abingdon Press, 1995).

2. The congregation organized primarily around the second of the two great commandments of Jesus is described in Lyle E. Schaller, *The Small Membership Church* (Nashville: Abingdon Press, 1994), pp. 23-40.

3. For this section and for the term "splintered attention," I am indebted to an essay by Peter F. Drucker, "The New Productivity Challenge," *Harvard Business Review*, November/December, 1991.

4. For another discussion of the three levels of change, see Lyle E. Schaller, *Strategies For Change* (Nashville: Abingdon Press, 1993), pp. 90-92.

5. For a pioneering, provocative, and persuasive argument that the electronic age has transformed public discourse, see Kathleen Hall Jamieson, *Eloquence in an Electronic Age* (New York: Oxford University Press, 1988).

11. *393 Diagnostic Questions*

1. For a provocative essay on this new category on the theological spectrum, see Roger E. Olson, "Postconservative Evangelicals," *The Christian Century*, May 3, 1995, pp. 480-86.

2. This distinction is discussed in greater detail in Lyle E. Schaller, *Looking in the Mirror* (Nashville: Abingdon Press, 1984), pp. 75-83.

3. For an elaboration of this point, see Lawrence N. Jones, "Timeless Priorities in Changing Contexts: African Americans and Denominationalism," Jackson Carroll and Wade Clark Roof, editors. *Beyond Establishment: Protestant Identity in a Post-Protestant Age* (Louisville: Westminster/John Knox Press, 1993), pp. 228-44.

4. For a provocative analysis of this trend, see W. Clark Gilpin, "The Theological Schools; Transmission, Transformation and Transcendence of Denominational Culture," in Ibid., pp. 188-203.

5. For a pioneering essay on the emerging role of denominational systems as regulatory bodies, see Craig Dykstra and James Hudnut-Beumler, "The National Organizational Structures of Protestant Denominations: An Invitation to a Conversation," Milton J. Coaler, et al., editors. *The Organizational Revolution* (Louisville: Westminster/John Knox, 1992), pp. 307-31.

6. The higher the level of trust in the laity and the greater the confidence in lay initiatives, the easier it is to launch off-campus ministries. The stronger the self-identified role of the regional judicatory as a regulatory body, the more difficult it is to launch and to staff with volunteers a variety of off-campus ministries. For a discussion of off-campus ministries, see Lyle E. Schaller, *Innovations in Ministry* (Nashville: Abingdon Press, 1994), pp. 64-133.

7. For additional examples of questions on specialized subjects, see Lyle E. Schaller, *44 Questions for Church Planters* (Nashville: Abingdon Press, 1991); Lyle E. Schaller, *Designing for Growth: Questions for Your Building Planning Committee* (Cleveland: United Church Board for Homeland Ministries, 1993).

12. What Happened to the Context?

1. See note 5 to chapter 11.

2. For a longer discussion of the differences between the East and the West, see Lyle E. Schaller, "Which Side of the River?" *The Clergy Journal*, July 1993.

3. A more detailed discussion of filling the vacuum is in Lyle E. Schaller, *Innovations in Ministry* (Nashville: Abingdon Press, 1994), pp. 37-46.

4. One group of those who hold out hope for the future of denominational systems believe it will be necessary to reinvent the organization. Another group contends that continuous quality improvement is the key. Michael Hammer symbolizes the first group while W. Edwards Deming is the symbol for the second. An excellent summary of those two positions is offered by Art Kleiner, "The Battle for the Soul of Corporate America," *Wired*, August 1995, pp. 122-73. A third group, and one that includes many senior pastors of very large congregations, has decided the prize in this battle is not worth the time and energy required to compete. They are concentrating their time and energy on strengthening the congregations they serve.